To Steven

Thank you *
your brillant teaching.
Thank to it, I could
write this book.

Smith

Shverlan, 15.704

With best,
all the best,
James

WHAT OTHERS ARE SAYING

"This book should be read by every military scholar because the issues addressed by Erick Labara are so important that they need to be discussed today."

Lucerne, March 31st 2004,
Major General Ulrich Zwygart, CO of the Armed Forces Senior
Cadre Training Center, Lucerne, Switzerland

"In this book you will find the thin red line between thinking about law in security politics, the importance of intelligence and finally the ultimate goal FREEDOM and PEACE for the world. You will get food for your brain and your stomach."

Lucerne, March 29th 2004,
Brigadier General Marcel Fantoni, CO of the General Staff School,
Lucerne, Switzerland

"Since September 11th 2001 global security concerns have dramatically risen. New emerging threats, such as transnational terrorism compel national and international authorities to enter in a challenging era. Corresponding new security concepts are vital for our civilization. With this book and his pragmatic approach, Erick Labara encourages us to think more intensely about preemption and prevention, and develops interesting conclusions. Moreover, I welcome the idea of integrating exquisite recipes and would like to recommend them warmly."

Lucerne, March 26th 2004,
Colonel GS Michael Arnold, Chief Doctrine in the Armed Forces
Senior Cadre Training Center, Lucerne, Switzerland

"I think Saddam Hussein's weapons of mass destruction are a threat, and that's why I voted to hold him accountable and to make certain that we disarm him. I think we need to, but it's not September 11th, folks, and the fact is that what we've learned is that the war on terror is much more of an intelligence operation and a law enforcement operation."[1]

Senator John F. Kerry

2004 Presidential Candidate

PREEMPTIVE WAR

ERICK LABARA

Global Security Press
An imprint of New Road Publishers
www.globalsecuritypress.com

PREEMPTIVE WAR
ERICK LABARA

Published by:
Global Security Press, an imprint of New Road Publishers, a James L. Clark company.

For more information please visit us online at:

- *http://www.globalsecuritypress.com*
- *http://www.newroadpublishers.com*
- *http://www.jameslclark.com*

For more information about the author, please visit his website at http://www.ericklabara.com. To access the recipes visit http://www.wonderfood.biz. The photographs of food presented in this book are © 2003 by Alain Besson and used with permission. The photographer may be contacted at *alain.besson@span.ch*.

Cover photograph of President Bush with Turkey © 2003 by Reuters. Used with permission.

Attention colleges and universities, corporations, and non-profit organizations: Quantity discounts are available on bulk purchases of this book for educational purposes, fund-raising, or gift giving. Special books, booklets, or book excerpts can also be created to fit your specific needs. For information, please contact the publisher online or call 1-877-552-5275.

Printed in the United States of America on acid free paper

10 9 8 7 6 5 4 3

Library of Congress Cataloging in Publication Data

Labara, Erick.
  Preemptive war / Erick Labara with James L. Clark. -- 1st ed. -- Washington, D.C. :
Global Security Press, 2004.
    p. cm.
    Includes bibliographical references.
    ISBN: 0972697578
    1. National security. 2. Military policy. 3. Strategy. 4. Defensive (Military science)
5. Military Sciences. 6. Current Affairs. I. Labara, Erick, 1963– . II. Clark, James L., 1972–   .
III. Title.

UA10.5 .L33 2004   2004104181
355/.03--dc22   0407

Preemptive War

An Analysis of International law, Diplomatic Issues and Intelligence

By

Erick Labara

Preface by Professor Richard Holmes

Foreword by Professor Christopher Bellamy

Another Perspective by Professor Albert A. Stahel

With contributions by James L. Clark

TABLE OF CONTENTS

ABOUT THE AUTHOR

Erick Labara was born in 1963 in Lausanne, Switzerland. After studying political and military sciences, he entered the Swiss Army as a professional artillery officer in 1988. He became General Staff officer in 1995, and was assigned to the G3 cell (operations) of a tank brigade.

From 1997 to 2000 he commanded an Artillery Battalion and returned to brigade staff in 2001 as Chief G2 (intelligence). In 2003 Erick Labara became the first Swiss Officer to earn a British Master of Science degree in Global Security from the Defence Academy of the United Kingdom at the Royal Military College of Science through Cranfield University under Professor Richard Holmes and Profesor Christopher Bellamy. Currently he works at the General Staff School; he holds the rank of lieutenant-colonel.

Erick Labara is an avid writer, former world champion and five-time Guinness Book of World Records holder in Sit-ups (1981), a pilot, 4th Dan black belt in Judo, and talented cook who enjoys fine gastronomy from all over the world.

"One way or the other, we are determined to deny Iraq the capacity to develop weapons of mass destruction and the missiles to deliver them. That is our bottom line."

President William Jefferson Clinton
February 4, 1998

ACKNOWLEDGEMENTS

The basic premises of this work are simple: assessing threats, waging a war and then building peace are not easy tasks. Today's understandings demand analytical qualities in order to draw relevant deductions and applicable consequences. I was lucky to have inherited this gift and to have learned this during my life and career. Therefore I would like to thank my parents and to express my sincere gratitude and respect to my former and current chiefs.

I am indebted to Professor Richard Holmes and Professor Christopher Bellamy from the Royal Military College of Science at the Defence Academy of the United Kingdom for providing me with very useful sources on which to base my study and for the important suggestions they made, for their preface and foreword respectively, and for their incredible enthusiasm and support.

To my friend James L. Clark; it was my distinct honor and privilege to meet and study with him at the Defence Academy of the United Kingdom where we both completed a Master of Science (MSc) degree in Global Security. It was James who advised me to publish this book and then played a significant role in its development by providing important and timely academic contributions, invaluable feedback, relevant ideas, superb content editing, and overall product development. Without his help, this book would not have been made a reality; I am very grateful. In fact, it is my sincere hope that he and I will collaborate in the near future on not only the second edition of this book but also on future works.

I wish to give special thanks to my friend Chou who meticulously corrected my English, syntax, and grammar.

I am also tremendously thankful for the feedback I received from Major General Ulrich Zwygart, Brigadier General Marcel Fantoni and Col (GS) Michael Arnold. They all gave freely of their time to read the draft versions of this book and gave me wonderful advice; thank you.

Special thanks also go out to Professor Albert A. Stahel, who wrote the "Another Perspective" after the foreword.

To my friend Alain Besson, who is a very talented photographer; his artistry brought my ideas to vivid color so I could share them with you in this book.

I simply cannot express how thankful I am for all of the help and encouragement that I received during this project. It is my sincere hope they will accept this final book favorably. The best comes from them, the shortcomings remain my own.

ABSTRACT

Individuals and nations who now continue to think and plan on the basis of security policies and strategies of the 1990s have not understood the message of September 11th 2001. The subsequent war against the Taliban Regime in Afghanistan called Operation 'Enduring Freedom', started on October 7th 2001 and was the beginning of a long lasting, world-wide mission involving several states' means for combating newly emerging threats. Thus, it was for certain that the twelve-year holiday of history (1990 - 2001) had come to an end.

The reform of strategic deterrence has gone through the alleged new doctrine of preemption. It has been the cause of major controversy and virulent debates in the international community, in the media and public especially at the end of 2002 and beginning of 2003, when the USA and the UK were threatening to wage a 'preemptive' war against Iraq. This issue came to its peak on March 20th 2003 when the US led armed forces launched military operations against the so-called rogue state of Iraq. Both the Bush administration and 10 Downing Street received considerable international condemnation. Understandably, and perhaps deliberately, the distinction between preemption, which has long been accepted in international law, and prevention, became confused.

The distinction between preemption and prevention is cardinal. The former could be perceived as an aggressive sword and the latter as a defensive shield, but such an approach is wrong. Indeed, preemption implies the imminence of a threat whereas prevention deals with a hostile danger, though not imminent. So prevention, of itself, is more aggressive than preemption. Preemption can be considered as a natural reflex, prevention as a response to a distant danger, a matter of foresight and free choice. This distinction, which contains elements of paradox, has not been understood and this had added to the confusion surrounding the casus belli for the recent war against Iraq manifested by quizzical ignoramuses.

In the light of the new emphasis on 'preemption', in the National Security Strategy of the United States of America, this distinction must be properly understood. If, in the future, democratic governments are to convince their peoples that they are going to war for the right reasons, they need to be honest and not to try to pass prevention as 'preemption.'

ABBREVIATIONS

ANC	African National Congress
CBRN	Chemical, Biological, Radiological and Nuclear
CIA	Central Intelligence Agency (US)
CNN	Cable News Network (US)
DIA	Defense Intelligence Agency (US)
DIS	Defence Intelligence Staff (UK)
DTRA	Defence Threat Reduction Agency
EEI	Essential Elements of Information
ELINT	Electronic Intelligence
FAPSI	Federal'noe agenstvo pravitelstvennoi svyazi informatsii (*Russian Federal Agency for Government Communications and Information*)
GCHQ	Government Communications Headquarters (UK)
GRU	Glavnoye Razvedyvatelnoye Upravlenie (*Russia: Russian military intelligence agency*)
HR	Human Rights

HUMINT	Human Intelligence
ICC	International Criminal Court
ICJ	International Court of Justice
IISS	International Institute for Strategic Studies
JARIC	Joint Air Photo Reconnaissance Centre (UK)
JIC	Joint Intelligence Committee (UK)
JSCSC	Joint Services Command and Staff College (UK)
KGB	Komitet Gosudarstvennoy Bezopasnosti (*USSR: Committee of State Security - Soviet Security and Foreign Intelligence Services (1954 - 1991)*)
Lt. Gen.	Lieutenant General
MI6	Secret Intelligence Services (UK), aka SIS
NATO	North Atlantic Treaty Organization
NRO	National Reconnaissance Office (satellite) (US)
NSA	National Security Agency (US)
NSS	National Security Strategy (US)
OSINT	Open Source Intelligence
SWAPO	South West Africa People's Organization

SC	Security Council
SIGINT	Signal Intelligence
SIS	See MI6
SVR	Sluzhba vneshnei razvedki (Russia: *Former KGB / Foreign Intelligence Service*)
TECHINT	Technical Intelligence
UK	United Kingdom
UN	United Nations
UNC	United Nations' Charter
UNSC	United Nations' Security Council
UNSCR	United Nations' Security Council Resolutions
USA	United States of America
USSR	Union of Soviet Socialist Republics
VX	Nerve Agent (ethyl-S-dimethylaminoethyl methylphosphonothiolate)
WMD	Weapons of Mass Destruction (see also CBRN)

"Without question, we need to disarm Saddam Hussein. He is a brutal, murderous dictator, leading an oppressive regime ... He presents a particularly grievous threat because he is so consistently prone to miscalculation ... And now he is miscalculating America's response to his continued deceit and his consistent grasp for weapons of mass destruction ... So the threat of Saddam Hussein with weapons of mass destruction is real."

Senator John F. Kerry (D, MA)
January 23, 2003

PUBLISHER'S NOTE

Like countless others around the world, the events of September 11th had a profound impact on me. Watching those planes slam into the Trade Towers, witnessing men and women jump to their deaths out of pure desperation in an attempt to avoid the flaming inferno consuming everything inside the building, seeing the gaping hole torn from the side of the Pentagon, and the smoldering field in Pennsylvania where the fourth aircraft crashed, filled my heart with a deep sorrow that I can hardly put into words.

Carl von Clausewitz astutely observed that war is not a mere act of policy, but a true political instrument; it is a continuation of political activity by other means.[1] As a soldier, there is a part of me that wants to join the armed forces again and be involved in the fight—if only to take justice, as it has been said, to those responsible for the terrible events of that day. However, there is another part of me that sympathizes with Dutch humanist Desiderius Erasmus' assessment that war is only delightful to those who have had no experience of it.[2] My personal decision was to forego engagement, at least at the tactical level, and instead focus my energy on broadening my understanding of the issues we are faced with today.

After finishing my MBA I applied to the Royal Military College of Science, which is part of the Defence Academy of the United Kingdom, to attend the Master of Science degree program in Global Security offered by Cranfield University's Department of Defence Management and Security Analysis, one of Europe's leading centers for both education and research in this field.[3] This post–graduate degree program, now in its fifth year, is run by the Security Studies Institute under the leadership of Professors Richard Holmes and Christopher Bellamy, and is aimed at generating an in-depth knowledge and understanding of what constitutes security in the 21st century.[4]

Nearly one year after 9/11 I walked into a room filled with twenty-plus men and women, most wearing their military dress uniforms, and sat down in a seat next to a remarkable Swiss Army officer named Erick Labara, the author of this book. His grasp of both military, and as you will see, culinary arts, is tremendous. He and I have since become very good friends and I consider myself as being privileged to know him.

During the course, we, along with colleagues from Ghana, Nepal, the United Kingdom, Thailand, the Czech Republic, Sierra Leone, China, and other nations were provided with an incredible opportunity to learn and grow. Areas of study included the development of military operations, doctrine and strategic thought; weapons of mass destruction, their control and verification; security, demography and the physical environment; and international law of war and the use of force. We traveled to Northern Ireland to learn about terrorism, sectarian violence, and organized crime, and to Normandy, France where we studied the D-Day invasion, one of the most significant battles of modern times. In fact, it was this trip that, quite independently, motivated both Erick and I to pursue our doctorates under Richard Holmes. Also, thanks to Professor Bellamy, a small group of us were able to visit St. Petersburg, Moscow, and Kursk to study the military policy of Russia and the former Soviet Union.

ERICK LABARA

As you might imagine, we also had to complete a significant academic thesis in order to graduate. My particular focus was on homeland security and Erick's was on preemptive and preventative war. After reading his thesis, I realized that others could benefit from his research and insight. Having recently become the controlling owner of a publishing company, I decided to approach Erick about turning his work into a proper publication. In December 2003, I started Global Security Press—named in honor of the program we had attended together—as an imprint and division of New Road Publishers; *Preemptive War* is the result of our creative collaboration.

The purpose of this book is simple: to feed the mind and body. It is intended to not only stir people to dialogue about the important issues we are faced with today, but also to inform and educate them. According to Plato,[5] education is not the practice of putting sight into blind eyes; it is the art of turning the soul from the shadows of ignorance towards the light of truth. And while the value of this book may not be nearly so weighty as Plato's theory may imply, his words do offer important insight on the study of this critical and timely topic. Far too often people look for quick–fix formulas as easy solutions to complex problems. While the idea may be an attractive one at first glance—especially to certain politicians and members of the media—it is entirely wrong. As General George Patton put it, "War is an art and as such is not susceptible of explanation by fixed formula."[6] Matters of critical importance such as preemption, prevention, and indeed even democracy, do not conform snugly into theoretical models, neat diagrams, and fancy flow charts. They do not fit neatly into the straightjacket of a single personal experience, theory, or historical study. And so it is with Global Security as a whole.

As the world seeks to cope with the challenges of the post 9/11 security environment, many issues have loomed large. On the national security side, the wisdom of pursuing a preemptive strategy is especially important today. When I attended law school we studied the Latin expression *caveat emptor*, "let the buyer beware," and how this concept applied to such areas as contract law. To some degree, it also applies to these topics.

In his address at West Point, on June 1st, 2002, President George W. Bush latently signaled to the world that the mere possession of so–called weapons of mass destruction by potentially hostile states would be grounds for anticipatory, or preventative war.[7] From a historical perspective, there has long been a clear distinction between preemption and prevention. The distinction is made by reference, as you will see in this book, to the notion of an immediate threat. Established both by customary international law and reaffirmed in the United Nations Charter, states have the unequivocal right to self defense. And while preemption is an extension of this right—if there is an imminent threat—States do not have an unqualified right to use unilateral force in international relations. Further, prevention in particular, which involves a military action in response to some putative future threat, is not widely considered a legitimate option. The presumption is that nations, such as the United States, have other ways of responding without resorting first to military force. This very concept is enshrined in the UN Charter[8] based on agreements such as the 1928 Kellogg-Briand Pact[9] and the 1945 Charter of the International Military Tribunal at Nuremberg.[10]

The United States' national strategy has always been a healthy blend of both defensive and offensive capabilities, which is a universally accepted norm adopted by virtually every state around the globe. In keeping with this tradition, the Bush Administration's willingness to entertain some preemptive measures is not a deviation from this. In fact, there is nothing new about America's occasional use of military preemption. Numerous presidential administrations, both Republican and Democrat, have not only ordered overt–military action in the Middle East since the end of World War II, but also directed covert action and even engaged in proxy wars.

The Bush administration's arguments in favor of a preemption are based on the view that warfare have changed. As Secretary of State Colin Powell has stated, "It's a different world... it's a new kind of threat."[11] And in many respects, war has changed. We now live in a world where asymmetry is the favored choice of those who wish to engage the United States without going head-to-head against our military. By hiding and blending into a populace, terrorists can—when the timing is right—launch devastating attacks such as flying airliners into buildings or setting off road-side improvised explosives as civilian convoys pass by. We face enemies today who "reject basic human values and hate the United States and everything for which it stands."[12] It is for this very reason that we have gone on the offensive. Indeed, after 9/11, many members of the Bush Administration began equating self defense with preemption:

> *"There is no question but that the United States of America has every right, as every country does, of self-defense, and the problem with terrorism is that there is no way to defend against the terrorists at every place and every time against every conceivable technique. Therefore, the only way to deal with the terrorist network is to take the battle*

to them. That is in fact what we're doing. That is in effect
self-defense of a preemptive nature."[13]

But the current administration's Middle East policy did not
emerge purely because of September 11th. It is a synthesis, if
you will, of the traditional concerns held by both Republican
and Democratic administrations since the end of World War
I, which has been largely focused on gaining control over the
oil in the Persian Gulf,[14] with the need to protect the American homeland from those groups who have a proven ability to
strike from within our own borders. Prior to September 11th,
this dichotomy did not exist. Like it or not, America's security
is currently linked—both economically and geopolitically—to
the security and stability of the Middle East. While I do not
personally hold that the war in Iraq was, or is, purely about oil,
to suggest that it does not play a significant role in our strategy
to "bring" democracy to the region would be ignorant. The reality is that about two-thirds of the world's known petroleum
reserves are in the Persian Gulf region. This constitutes "a
stupendous source of strategic power, and one of the greatest
material prizes in world history."[15] Saudi Arabia is the largest
single depository of oil reserves, with about 21 percent of the
known world total. But, Iraq, which we now control, is number
two on that list with about 11 percent.[16]

The British Empire, the predecessor to the current American
"Empire" now being built in the region, got underway with
the occupation of Aden in 1839.[17] After suffering a devastating defeat to South Yemeni guerillas fighting for their independence in 1967, Britain announced that it would withdraw
its forces from east of Suez by the end of 1971. During the
same period America was suffering similar defeats in South

Vietnam. The Tet offensive,[18] launched in 1968 by the National Liberation Front of South Vietnam, made it clear to the world that the United States would not quell the determination of the Vietnamese people fiercely dedicated to overcoming—what to them—was nothing more then American aggression. These two events prompted the Nixon Administration to develop a strategy to defend American interests in Islamic oil-producing states such as Saudi Arabia and Kuwait, against the "threat" of secular Arab nationalism such as that lead by Egypt's then President Gamal Abdul Nasser, and the Ba'ath party regimes of, ironically, Iraq and Syria.

In the summer of 1969, the Nixon-Kissinger doctrine was released, which relied upon the formation of so–called "re-gional–influentials" to preserve American interests. This "twin-pillar" policy was composed of Saudi Arabia and Iran who purchased large amounts of weaponry from the United States with cash profits from oil. This doctrine was carried by Ford and Carter, but with the Iranian Revolution and Soviet invasion of Afghanistan in 1979, came to an abrupt end. These changes raised new concerns about Soviet intentions at the same time Middle Eastern oil was becoming more important to America's economic strength. In response, Carter estab-lished a "Rapid Deployment Force" capable of direct military intervention in the Persian Gulf. In his 1980 State of the Union address Carter stated:

> *"An attempt by any outside force to gain control of the Per-sian Gulf region would be regarded as an assault on the vital interests of the United States. And such an assault would be repelled by any means necessary, including mili-tary force."* [19]

Carter and his successor, Ronald Reagan, proceeded to engage in regional proxy wars. First, America supported Iraq when it attacked Iran in 1980, and then to the Mujahideen who were fighting to expel the Soviets. During his presidency, Reagan continued to build America's war fighting capability with a focus on direct military intervention in the Middle East. In 1983 he transformed the Rapid Deployment Force into the Central Command.[20] Further, Casper Weinberger, Reagan's Secretary of Defense, forwarded the policy that the United States should be willing to introduce its forces into the region should it even appear that access to Persian Gulf oil might be threatened.[21]

Units from Central Command fought in both the 1991 and 2003 Gulf Wars lead by Presidents Bush. In fact, it was these wars that overcame the reluctance of Persian Gulf oil states to allow the United States to have military bases in the region. Since 1990 we have had an increasing number of installations, which by all accounts appear to be permanent, being built throughout the region. Having a solid presence in the area provides America with a greater ability to directly intervene to secure its interests in the Middle East. However, the war in 1990 did not produce the so-called "New World Order" that it was supposed to. The betrayal of the Shi'ites and the Kurds who rose up against Saddam Hussein after being called upon to do so by the first President Bush was a clear indicator that the United States, at the time, was not willing to radically alter the region's geo-political make up. Democracy in the region posed a real threat to conservative oil-producing states since, theoretically, the common people would have been allowed to vote and radically change policy. Additionally, the idea of independence for the Iraqi Kurds was then, and remains today, a threat to America's NATO ally Turkey.

ERICK LABARA

Interestingly, in 1992, Paul Wolfowitz, who was then number three in the former President Bush Pentagon, and is now number two in the current Bush Pentagon, wrote in his "Defense Planning Guidance"[22] a policy that proposed preemptive war on a massive scale for global domination. He indicated that American-styled democracy was applicable everywhere in the world and should be exported, if necessary, by force. After it was leaked to the media, the former President Bush ordered that it be rewritten. There is no question that today, especially after the events of September 11th that this document, or at least the theory behind it, is playing a heavy role in this Administration's direction in the Middle East. But it is also true that the Clinton Administration followed this line of thought. For example, during the mid-1990s William Kristol, Director of the Project for a New American Century, successfully lobbied the government to pass the Iraq Liberation Act in 1998.[23] The Clinton Administration made it very clear that disarmament by itself was insufficient and that a regime change was needed. In December of 1998, Operation Desert Fox was launched, which according to the Defense Department was designed to "...degrade Saddam Hussein's ability to make and to use weapons of mass destruction, to diminish [his] ability to wage war against his neighbors [and] to demonstrate to Saddam Hussein the consequences of violating international obligations."[24] But it was really September 11th which opened the door for the United States to begin implementing the doctrine first articulated by Paul Wolfowitz nearly a decade before.

In *Summa Theoligica* Thomas Aquinas wrote, "A just war is apt to be described as one that avenges wrongs, when a nation or state has to be punished, for refusing to make amends for the wrongs inflicted by its subjects..."[25] In this sense, there was a moral imperative demanding action. While I would have preferred that the international community, in the form of the United Nations, had taken collective action against Saddam Hussein and the Taliban, rather than placating them for so many years, I accept that there comes a point where someone must do something; some action, rather than discussion, must take place. The task ultimately fell to the United States and the *Coalition of the Willing*. Ultimately, one must decide for themselves whether preemption or prevention is right or wrong, just or unjust. That is part of the purpose behind this work: to get you thinking about it. But either way, one thing is for certain—there are incredible costs associated with taking the lead. For instance, the preemptive and preventive invasions of Afghanistan and Iraq, respectively, may be setting a precedent which could be potentially disastrous; the possibility exists that other nations will follow suit in using unilateral military action in other conflicts and regions around the globe. However, some might say that I am missing the point entirely—that preemption and prevention are but tools being used by the United States in pursuit of its real goal: to build a new American empire. If our goal is only to "export democracy," as Paul Wolfowitz and his ideological followers assert, then it may be worth considering the experiences of the British Empire before we travel too far down that path.

At its height, between 1815 and 1914, the British Empire was the largest exporter of manufactured goods and the largest importer of raw materials from the rest of the world. They controlled the seas, but not the globe. Where they did have control, they cleverly maintained it through indirect rule. That is, they used a system where local intermediaries did their bidding. They had no intention of exporting their political system, because to do so, would have required far too much involvement at the local level by the British and an enormous infusion of troops and money, which would have been economically, socially, and politically unwise.[26]

In 2001 Afghanistan became, what could be argued, the first nation to find itself under imperial rule by the United States. The current interim President, Hamid Karzai, has no real power outside Kabul, and it may very well be decreasing with each passing day. Many of the warlords are now back in power over their provinces and Afghanistan is, once again, the leading source of opium production in the world. The establishment of post–war democratic institutions in Afghanistan is proving difficult to say the least. Remember, Afghanistan was not so much an example of state-backed terrorism as it was of a terrorism backed state. Thus, building (not rebuilding) the country is a task that will take generations, not just few months or even a few years. Iraq is hardly different in this respect. It will be a considerable time before its infrastructure is restored to the pre–modern state it was before the war started, let alone to one which is capable of provide its citizens with the basic stability they have a right to expect and which is essential to economic and social progress. The problem of institution building has to be addressed if we are to prevent future conflicts. To me, it is questionable if democracy will take root in either location.

President George W. Bush declared, "All Iraqis must have a voice in the new government, and all citizens must have their rights protected."[27] In theory, I support this concept. As members of a prosperous society built on a democratic foundation, we Americans innately believe that what we have would also be good for the rest of the world. Democracy, after all, has become associated with freedom. But democracy is not limited by some intrinsic inclination to a common appreciation for the respect of individuals or the freedoms they desire. In political theory, democracy encompasses something much more general: majority rule. Unfortunately, majority rule is often synonymous with popularity, which does not itself assure either democracy or freedom. The assumption that real exercisable, individual freedom and centralized, political or governmental control can coexist as a hybrid social system—the *sine qua non* of what we have come to recognize as the modern liberal democracy—is not only contradictory, but it is also an impractical and potentially dangerous concept to forward. There are countless historical examples of what happens when the majority rules and the unpopular minority does not. Further, whatever the original definitions, democracy no longer exists separate from the free market—they are inextricably linked.

One thing is for certain, the costs associated with a transition to democracy can, and will be, enormously high—not only in terms of economics, but also socially. Consider the former communist states for just a moment if you require proof. I am not saying that democracy itself is necessarily the wrong choice, but I do wonder if it will "work" in Iraq and Afghanistan as it has in post-WWII Germany and Japan. Remember, it is now a truism that what is most important is not a country's first election, but rather its second, third, and fourth. And what matters most is not simply that people have the right to vote, but that they are offered a fair and honest choice under conditions that are truly free. This is hard to accomplish, even in America. It is an interesting dichotomy to be sure that begs the question: is there an alternative? I do not know, to be honest. Perhaps there is something far more feasible and much more likely to guarantee national stability and cohesiveness in these countries, but democracy is the best we have to offer. It is all we know. But still, skeptics abound. Adam Garfinkle, for example, a Senior Fellow at the Foreign Policy Research Institute, argues that trying to build democracy in the Arab world will not only fail, but will also stir anti-Americanism.[28] The vision most often conjured by the critics of installing democracy in Iraq and Afghanistan, is that of a violent societies where civil unrest reins supreme, rival tribes seek revenge on one another, and the our military tramples the country and abuses their people. To some degree, we are seeing manifestations of this, albeit to a far lesser degree than was predicted.

Suggesting that this process will be easy is myopic at best. Deposing the Taliban and Saddam Hussein was but one part of a very complex puzzle that cannot be solved overnight. But now that we are in these countries, interest and obligation alike require us to make sure that there is a transfer of power to some form of Arab democracy as soon as possible. The price of failure would likely be much higher than the cost of transition itself. Without a transition, it is likely that both Afghanistan and Iraq will remain permanently occupied, degenerate back to terror-breeding failed states, or fall under the control of new dictatorships that are no better than the old ones. Any of these outcomes would be disastrous for America's interests and reputation. Success, on the other hand, could bring immense rewards. Not only would the international community be joined by stable and productive countries, but they would serve as working examples of unique Arab democracies, which other Arabs might come to respect, admire, and seek to emulate on their own accord without pressure—or God forbid—more preemption or prevention. While these countries may be far from the ideal fertile soil needed for growing democracy, it would be foolish to underestimate the impact that a determined United States can have on this effort.

Otto von Bismarck once remarked that "Fools say that they learn by experience. I prefer to profit by others' experience."[29] And while I would generally agree that "the best defense is a good offense," *caveat preemptor*—let the preemptor beware.

James L. Clark
Washington, DC
May 20, 2004

1. Carl Von Clausewitz, *On War*, Edited by Anatol Rapoport, 1982, Viking Press
2. Desiderius Erasmus, *The Adages of Erasmus*, by William Barker, 2002, University of Toronto Press
3. See http://www.defenceacademy.mod.uk/ for more information
4. See http://www.cranfield.ac.uk/prospectus/shrivenham/gs.cfm for more information
5. Plato, *The Republic*, 2000, Dover Publications
6. See http://www.military-quotes.com/Patton.htm
7. See http://www.whitehouse.gov/news/releases/2002/06/20020601-3.html
8. See http://www.un.org/aboutun/charter/
9. See http://www.yale.edu/lawweb/avalon/imt/kbpact.htm
10. See http://www.yale.edu/lawweb/avalon/imt/proc/imtconst.htm
11. Colin Powell, *Perspectives: Powell Defends a First Strike as Iraq Option*, interview with the New York Times, September 8, 2002, sec. 1, p. 18.
12. The National Security Strategy of the United States of America, September 2002
13. Donald H. Rumsfeld, See http://www.defenselink.mil/news/Oct2001/t10292001_t1028sd3.html.
14. Pirouz Mojtahed-Zadeh, Peireuz Mujtahidzeadah, *Security and Territoriality in the Persian Gulf*, 1999, Curzon Press
15. Foreign Relations of the United States, 1945, Government Printing Office, vol. 8, p. 45
16. *Oxford Atlas of the World*, 10th Edition, 2002
17. See http://www.worldstatesmen.org/Yemen.html
18. See http://www.pbs.org/wgbh/amex/vietnam/107ts.html
19. See http://www.jimmycarterlibrary.org/documents/speeches/su79jec.phtml
20. See http://www.centcom.mil/aboutus/centcom.htm
21. Congressional Research Service, *Petroleum Imports from the Persian Gulf: Use of U.S. Armed Force to Ensure Supplies*, May 26, 1981, CRS Issue Brief 79046, p. 1
22. See http://www.pbs.org/wgbh/pages/frontline/shows/iraq/etc/wolf.html
23. See http://www.library.cornell.edu/colldev/mideast/libera.htm
24. See http://www.defenselink.mil/specials/desert_fox/
25. St. Thomas Aquinas, *Summa Theologica*, II-II, Question 40, "On War", 1947, Benziger Brothers
26. Frank McDonough, *The British Empire, 1815-1914*, 2000, National Textbook Company
27. See http://www.whitehouse.gov/news/releases/2003/03/20030301.html
28. Adam Garfinkle, *The Impossible Imperative? Conjuring Arab Democracy*, 2002, The National Interest
29. See http://www.military-quotes.com/otto-von-bismarck.htm

Erick Labara

PREFACE

By Richard Holmes, PhD, Professor of Military Science and Doctrine, Cranfield University, Defence Academy of the UK

Swiss army officers had not been common features of my life as a university teacher, but I very soon warmed to Erick Labara. Partly it was his intellectual grasp of professional issues; partly his ability to sustain a heavy work-load (I now understand why my Swiss watch never lets me down); and partly his eye for the ground, which I discovered early on in the course when we were standing, on an unseasonably warm October day, atop the German strongpoint Hillman just behind the Normandy coast. But it was not until much later in the course that I discovered another virtue. He is an exceptional cook, reliable yet inventive, with the ability to engage a particular dish with just the right wine, almost as if this was an artillery fire-plan rather than an elegant dinner-table.

The one thing I can say without fear of contradiction is that this book is wholly original, for the notion of folding recipes into a work on one of the pressing issues of our age is a novel one. But in a sense it brings together both sides of its author's temperament: intellectual analysis and practical creativity. I leave it for readers to judge the recipes for themselves, although, given that their creator's cooking has never disappointed, I should be surprised if they failed.

It is with the book's main content that this preface is chiefly concerned. Erick Labara poses a straightforward challenge to those whose thinking is firmly rooted in the post-Treaty of Westphalia world and reject unilateral preemptive military action. He argues, in words that echo those of many men who stand on the threshold of genuinely revolutionary situations, that we simply cannot go on as we are. But what is to be done? His study goes to the heart of the thorny issues of pre-emption and anticipatory self-defence. The former, he argues, is 'justified by an imminent and real threat of attack, a clear present danger...' and this is a conclusion from which few would now dissent. Preventive war, on the other hand, is far less well-regarded by the international community because the threat is neither imminent nor well-focused, and while pre-emption is a 'natural reflex' against a threat, prevention seems altogether more aggressive.

Erick Labara argues, on the basis of number of historical case studies, that there are times when preventive war can indeed be justified. In the case of the 2003 Gulf war, most controversially, he argues that the coalition attack on Iraq met most of the traditional criteria of Just War.

He is too astute not to acknowledge that 'the risks of escalation or precipitation are very high,' and stresses the vital role of intelligence in helping establish whether the proposed operation will actually eliminate the threat targeted. In his analysis of intelligence sources he rightly emphasises the importance HUMINT, and of what he terms 'investigative intelligence' though he recognizes the difficulty of finding personnel with the skills (which need to include languages and cultural understanding) for these crucial tasks. He concludes that 'anticipatory self-defence could be perceived as the lesser of two evils and so, depending on the circumstances, be formally permitted' and proposes a hypothetical United Nations Charter article which would help define these circumstances.

Erick Labara's logic is unlikely to commend itself to those who approach the challenges of the Twenty-First Century from a traditional standpoint. Yet the uncomfortable fact remains that these challenges will neither go away of their own accord, nor can they be properly dealt with by the apparatus of law and doctrine currently available. He is right to suggest that they demand a collective solution, and no less so to warn of the danger of individual responses which might make things worse rather than better. Preventive war may indeed be something which many will prefer to regard as unthinkable. But it cannot be right, in terms of the simplest natural justice, for a state to be compelled to wait before acting until it risks receiving a devastating first blow.

Whether readers agree with Labara's arguments is not the real issue of this book. That issue is the certainty that the world cannot go on as it is without a substantial risk that weapons of mass destruction will be used, not as people like me feared, half a lifetime ago, as part of an East-West conflict, but as part of an asymmetric struggle fuelled by complex cultural ingredients. This threat is, in a sense, as real and present whether one lives in Birmingham, Baltimore or Bern. And if this book at least encourages us to think more deeply about our response, then its author will have succeeded.

Richard Holmes
Shrivenham, England
December 2003

"We know that he [Saddam] has stored secret supplies of biological and chemical weapons throughout his country."

Former Vice President Al Gore
September 23, 2002

FOREWORD

By Chris Bellamy, PhD, Professor of Military Science and Doctrine, Cranfield University, Defence Academy of the UK

This book addresses a cardinal question in Security Studies at the start of the Third Millennium. With the end of the Cold War and the bi-polar balance of force and terror, the role of international law in assuring security has become even more important than in the preceding three centuries. With only one superpower - or hyper power – security can only be assured by a system of international law accepted and respected by all responsible nation states. Rather than using pure force – or the pure threat of force – to ensure order, force can now only be legitimate as a sanction within the system of international law. In domestic law, punishment and coercion - or the threat of punishment and coercion - is the last resort in enforcing laws which most people obey. Similarly, in the 21st century, national, international, regional and global security will depend, above all, on creating a proper and workable relationship between international law, strategy, diplomacy and development.

Since the Caroline case in 1837 the right of States to launch pre-emptive strikes - that is, strikes to head off, deflect or mitigate attacks that are 'overwhelming' and 'imminent' - has been widely accepted in international law. The right to launch preventive attacks - attacks on a target which may become a threat in the future, but which does not pose an 'overwhelming' or 'imminent' threat right now, is far more uncertain.

From the 1930s, when Stanley Baldwin famously warned that 'the bomber will always get through', policies of deterrence were attractive.[1] 'If you start a fight you will suffer out of all proportion to anything you can hope to gain.' But now we face potential adversaries who are not going to be deterred. 'Asymmetric', or, more correctly, 'dissymmetric' adversaries who do not share our values, our vulnerabilities, our respect for human life. As the United States national security strategy now recognizes, pre-emption may be the only way to deflect what deterrence cannot now achieve. 'Go out and find them before they can do something to you'.

But pre-emption is not the same as prevention. 'Preventive war' is about attacking somebody who is not (yet) in a position to launch an imminent or overwhelming strike. Is preventive war legal? The international law of war and armed conflict recognizes two separate but interrelated concepts. *Jus ad bellum* - going to war for the right reasons. And *jus in bello* - waging war in the most humane way possible, given that war is a last and terrible resort, when all attempts at reasonable discourse have failed. The distinction between preemptive and preventive war is the most important jus ad bellum issue of our time.

In the run-up to the 2003 campaign in Iraq the distinction between pre-emption and prevention was imperfectly made. Using a clear differentiation between the two, it is easy to see how the British and US Governments may, unconsciously, perhaps, have sought to portray the threat posed by Iraqi chemical and biological weapons as more 'overwhelming' and 'imminent' than it really was, thus justifying war on the grounds of pre-emption, rather than prevention. With hindsight, it seems the war was more the latter - but the case for such a war, in customary international law, is far more difficult to make. As this book demonstrates, many of the 'preventive' campaigns and wars in history look pretty offensive.

I became interested in what constitutes a 'defensive' strategy some 15 years ago when I was writing my PhD under the late John Erickson at Edinburgh University. In the prevailing atmosphere of glasnost' and what had earlier been called détente, two Soviet analysts had produced an analysis of 'defensive' options available to the Soviet Union to replace the rather intimidating stance adopted by the Bear hitherto.[2] These ranged from preemptive strike - not very defensive, really - through an initial defensive followed by a massive counter attack, for which the Battle of Kursk, 60 years ago this year, was a model. Then came an offensive, but limited to the area which had previously been and was rightfully yours, modeled on the Battle of Khalkin Gol in 1939. Finally, there was a 'defensive defense'—a Maginot line strategy. I cannot help thinking that if those gentlemen were writing now they would have had to insert a fifth, even more apparently offensive option before the pre-emptive strike, and that would be 'preventive war'.

I was therefore delighted when Erick Labara, a guest of ours from Switzerland, chose to address this question in a dissertation which he completed as part of our Master of Science degree in Global Security at Cranfield University's Shrivenham campus. And who better to address it than a Swiss? It must be remembered that the Swiss, whose historic military reputation is formidable, have retained their independence and avoided the scourge of war which has lapped about their mountainous frontiers for hundreds of years. How? Because they take the business of defence very seriously. Hitler would no doubt have liked to take Switzerland. But in Switzerland's case - unlike any other neighbor's - deterrence clearly worked. From their neutral position, the Swiss have been able to play a major part in the international control of excess in war—*jus in bello*—through the

Red Cross, and host important organs of the United Nations.

The principal joy of teaching—at any level—is the true fulfillment of the word 'education' in its original Latin meaning. 'To lead out'. Not to be prescriptive, or to 'cram' the student with knowledge for the minor tactical objective of passing an examination. Knowledge that, sadly, but perhaps inevitably, will be forgotten as fast as it has been acquired. No. To spot, even to sense, remarkable ability and talent. To nurture, to encourage abilities and talents of which the student, him- or herself, may be unaware. At the postgraduate level the 'students', collectively and individually, may bring to bear a wealth of maturity, experience and knowledge which exceeds that, collectively and individually, of the 'teachers'. Tact and diplomacy are required when dealing with customers who are people of great professional competence, sophistication and cosmopolitan experience, not to mention seniority in their own nations' armed forces. People like Erick.

It was on our field trip to Northern Ireland that I first became aware that Erick was a gourmet, and a connoisseur of wine. During the weekend in the middle of the trip, after a very demanding week, the course takes a well-earned break. Securely battened down against the wind, the cold and the dark behind stone walls in what had been a fortified farmhouse he asked if I would share a good bottle of wine with him, to go with the excellent dinner. 'You choose', I said. The price tag of the bottle he chose took me aback, but from then on we recognized a mutual conviction. 'If you're going to do it, do it properly'. Later, at the Wiltshire farmhouse where he stayed while studying with us, he invited many of his colleagues to the most superb dinners, me and Heather, my wife, included.

I was therefore delighted to have the opportunity to write a foreword for this unique book. Erick was understandably curious about what our reaction would be to a book combining an examination of the evolving law of armed conflict with cooking. I can think of nothing more appropriate. There are many similarities between gastronomy—the art and science of food—and polemology—the art and science of war. The origins of both are lost in the mists of time but both were clearly developed by the time of the first civilizations which were attended, unfortunately, by the dark side of civilization. Organized warfare for political ends. Ancient murals invariably depict conquest and capture alongside feasting and victory celebrations. The most proficient at war were equally proficient at feasting. The Romans, for example.

This theme has continued throughout history. As I write this foreword, in November 2003, the newspapers are full of the headline 'The Turkey has landed', a reference to President George W Bush's flying visit to US troops in Iraq to spend a couple of hours with them at Thanksgiving. Great military commanders always understood the importance of rations. 'An army marches on its stomach', as Napoleon reportedly said. Food is not just essential to maintain physical strength and endurance, but also for morale purposes. A good, tasty meal, especially one that evokes some positive element of the soldier's upbringing and family background, will have far more of an effect on the moral component of fighting power than the same scientific mix of proteins, carbohydrates and fats delivered in a boring or unappetizing form.

Furthermore there are many parallels between the art and science of food and nutrition and the art and science of war. Everything in war, as Clausewitz said, 'is very simple. But the simplest thing is very difficult'.[3] So with gastronomy. The principles of strategy can be understood by a child. Hit him where he is weakest, hit him when he isn't looking. It is doing it, at the right place, at the right time, which is difficult. Similarly, in gastronomy, there are but a few tastes—sweet, sour, salt... But they can be combined in an infinite number of ways. The very elements of fighting power—the moral, the physical and the conceptual—are mirrored in the components of a good meal. Respectively, I would suggest, the appearance and presentation (moral); the textures (physical); and the handful of flavors combined in infinite varieties (conceptual).

The parallels go further. During the First World war, images of eating were commonplace to describe how forces had to chew, or gnaw, their way through defences. To get to the vitals of the enemy one had to work from the outside in, like a conventional oven. But with the advent of air power, and even more so in the modern era, the digital era, we hear of attacking an enemy 'inside out'. Of striking at the centre of gravity first, using modern technology, including electronic and information warfare, and then watching as the rest of the target collapses around it. That approach was key to the US plan 1003 Victor to dismantle Iraq in 2003.

Is it coincidence that the ability to do this coincided with - or followed slightly behind—the appearance of the microwave oven, which cooks—from the inside out? Warfare has now moved into the microwave era. Micro waving has its attractions, in terms of speed and convenience, but not everyone has a microwave—yet, and not every recipe is suitable for micro waving. Professional chefs, I hear, use the microwave, among other things, to ensure butter is at the right temperature. Again the analogy is clear: 'inside-out' is a useful tool, but it can never replace or supplant more conventional means, which must be applied as well.

Erick's examination of the concepts of pre-emption and prevention also mirror the ideals of nutrition. Slow-burning carbohydrates to sustain the body and prevent exhaustion. Infinitely preferable to the hasty insertion of glucose and other preventive action as the blood sugar drops too low—analogous to reacting only after someone has launched an attack.

There are also parallels between key military technologies and cooking. Making a nuclear bomb was once considered an unlikely possibility. Like the famous challenge to a famous chef to 'bake ice-cream'. The chef solved the problem. In Baked Alaska, meringue is placed around the ice–cream to provide superb insulation, enabling the casing to cook while protecting the ice–cream inside. Similarly, in a nuclear weapon, a 'tamper' around the outside contains the nuclear reaction inside for long enough to cause an explosion, preventing the fissile material from fragmenting too quickly.

And in gastronomy, as in war, some things are counter-intuitive. Bombing people to break their will may have the opposite effect. Similarly, who would think that the bitter–sour tasting onion, when fried in salty butter, would create sweetness? Yet it does…

But Erick would not have been able to bring his culinary delights to the reader's attention had he not also had a critical eye for photography. Thus, he has shared his culinary passion with the talented photographer Alain Besson, whose works are included in this book. This underlines the importance of imagery, in matters culinary as well as military. I find that many students to not think graphically, and fail to understand, or do not appreciate, the importance of imagery. On the degree, we make sure they learn. Security and strategic studies, military history, or whatever you want to call it, is a superbly visual, graphic subject. Imagery is crucial to intelligence and to Battle Damage Assessment. I was once shown the notebook of one Boris

Shaposhnikov, a student at the Russian General Staff Academy before World War I, who later became a Marshal of the Soviet Union and Chief of the General Staff at the outbreak of the Great Patriotic war in 1941. It was full of the most intricate and carefully drawn diagrams of ancient battles, immaculately delineated in coloured pencil. Officers used to be taught to sketch, draw and paint—a part of their education and training now, sadly, discarded. The diagrams in Erick's assignments diagrams reminded me of Shaposhnikov's. Maybe his career will prosper similarly?

As a military historian, I am also aware of the enormous popularity of history—especially military history—with the general public in bookshops and on television. Military history has been described as 'the new gardening'. It certainly vies with gardening, and cooking, as a subject of popular interest. Ground and terrain have always been a key part of military operations—as have food and logistics. So why not combine the disciplines?

That said, the issues of international law which Erick Labara explores are deadly serious and of enormous significance for global security. They are combined with lighter, gastronomic, relief, like the tragic and the comic in a great Shakespeare play. And that, surely, is a pretty good model.

Chris Bellamy
London, England
November 2003

1. House of Commons, November 10th 1932.

2. Andrei Kokoshin and Maj Gen Valentin Larionov, Extract from the book *Problems of Preventing War*, in *Mirovaya Ekonomika I Mezhdunarodnye Otnosheniya* (World Economy and International Affairs), 6/1988, pp. 23-31.

3. Carl von Clausewitz, *Vom Kriege* (On War), ed.and trans. Michael Howard and Peter Paret, (Princeton UP, 1976), Bk. 1, Ch. 7, 'Friction in War', p. 119.

ERICK LABARA

ANOTHER PERSPECTIVE

By Dr. Albert A. Stahel, Professor of Strategic Studies, Military Academy of the ETH, Zürich, Switzerland

In the fifties and sixties of the twentieth century various publications provided new impulses to the strategic thinking in the USA. The Americans Albert Wohlstetter and Herman Kahn introduced a new definition of "deterrence" for the nuclear age between the USA and the USSR. Deterrence was thus defined as the capability to launch a devastative nuclear counter-strike against hostile territory in response to an enemy attack.

The credibility of nuclear deterrence should not only be based on the availability of the respective weapons systems but should also be determined by the political intention and will to use such weapons. Operational readiness of nuclear weapons was achieved through preparations for a preemptive attack, a preemptive strike or a preventive war. These terms had then become parts of the strategic vocabulary. By means of these two differing concepts the nuclear deterrence as a function of a retaliatory capability was linked with the political will to engage in a preemptive and preventive war and thus the capability to wage a nuclear war. This state of affairs was not openly communicated in the USA. Only with the end of the Cold War did these political scruples disappear. This may explain the reason why the Bush Administration introduced in 2002 the preemptive war as part of their strategy and, by blurring the distinction between preemptive and preventive strikes, consciously signaled their willingness to use preventive wars against any discredited dictator.

Already in the seventies the Europeans realized that the American definition of deterrence could not apply to all the States and thus was not universally applicable. Armed forces of smaller States were at best capable of repelling an attack or fighting a war of attrition. That is the reason why, in the early seventies, the American Horst Mendershausen brought up the difference between offensive and defensive deterrence. The offensive deterrence was meant to be a function of the retaliatory capability whereas the defensive deterrence was a function of the defensive capability.

In a small country such as Switzerland military preparations could only be focused on defensive deterrence. Its geographical situation in Europe, its mountainous terrain shaped by rivers and valleys as well as its tradition of neutrality gave Switzerland no other choice than to defend itself in a defensive rather than offensive way. This was the task the Swiss Armed Forces focused on over decades. Their concept was a territorial area defence reinforced by a network of fortresses and obstacles. Only after the demise of the Soviet Union, did the Swiss gradually abandon this tradition.

Any Swiss, officer or citizen, who was influenced by this military tradition, is still committed to the spirit of defence and neutrality. Political or military interference in the interests of other States is still a thing my generation is unwilling to do. For my generation only, the defence of our fatherland can be a just war. It is therefore unusual for a middle-aged Swiss such as me to see that Erick Labara designates the US-led operations such as Iraqi Freedom to be a just war. For a Swiss like me, who is committed to the tradition of his country, the wars led by the Bush Administration can never be considered just wars. I therefore admire Erick Labara's courage to carry out this analysis. He has chosen the "not so easy" scientific approach. This said, I would never allow myself to play down his scientific achievement, on the contrary.

I wish Erick Labara all the best for his future as well as for his culinary skills.

Prof. Dr. Albert A. Stahel
Zürich, Switzerland
March, 2004

"We have known for many years that Saddam Hussein is seeking and developing weapons of mass destruction."

Senator Ted Kennedy (D, MA)
September 27, 2002

CHAPTER ONE

INTRODUCTION

'The strong do what they have the power to do and the weak accept what they have to accept.'[2]

Thucydides (460 - 399 BC)

INTRODUCTION

Despite widespread opposition both at home and abroad, the Bush administration was trying to convince the United States (US) Congress, the public and the international community about the necessity of an American intervention in Iraq. Such an action was considered to be an unprecedented use of force within a new doctrine: 'military preemption.' On June 1st 2002, George W. Bush, the 43rd President of the United States of America (USA) delivered a speech at West Point in front of a floor of new graduates unveiling the outline for the Nation's new national security strategy. He said: 'Our security will require all Americans to be forward-looking and resolute, to be ready for preemptive action when necessary to defend our liberty and to defend our lives.'[3] From that point forward, the United States has the option to lead preemptive first-strike actions against any nation or organization seen as an eminent or potential threat, including those who have acquired Weapons of Mass Destruction (WMD).[4]

Indeed, 'with the publication of its new National Security Strategy document in September 2002, the Bush administration has elevated "military preemption" against so-called "rogue states" and terrorist groups to official US doctrine.'[5] As deterrence and containment were considered to be the American strategy during the Cold War, preemption has supplanted this concept. Consequently, this new doctrine allows the USA to wage war against states which are perceived as hostile to American interests.

Does it mean that facing the new threats, preemption leads

to the fossilization of strategic deterrent capabilities? Apparently not, as Secretary of State Colin Powell has asserted, '[P]reemption has long been part of the panoply of American defense instruments and deterrence is not dead.'[6] It thus remains part of a spectrum of approaches, including non-military instruments, which the US will continue to use as a policy option. If Iraq has been the first target of this new doctrine, its application goes beyond the bounds of the 'Axis of Evil' drawn by the Bush Administration. Indeed, military forces and intelligence services alike need to be radically transformed. However, the conditions under which this new doctrine would be undertaken remained hazy.

There are numerous examples where the great powers, through discretionary political opportunities, have chosen infringements to be sanctioned and sanctions to be imposed by the international community. Self defense, for example, cannot be invoked in order to initiate a military intervention against another state whose aggression is not obvious. A simple and minor border incident cannot justify a generalized armed conflict. Nevertheless, in international experience and practice, some states already seem to have extensively interpreted the right of self defense: for example, an ordinary maritime hitch was one factor which provoked war between the US and North Vietnam.[7] In June 1981, 'Israel attacked and destroyed a nuclear reactor nearing completion in Iraq, justifying its conduct on the grounds of anticipatory self defense'[8] and professed that this reactor located in Tuwaitha (see Appendix A-2) would be used to manufacture weapons against the Israeli state.

As a consequence of the rise of transnational terrorism, the doctrine of preemption forms the logical evolution of US efforts to thwart the proliferation of WMD. In 1998, the founding of the Defence Threat Reduction Agency (DTRA), which deals comprehensively with threats of the proliferation and use of WMD, had notably led to research studying new means capable of neutralizing underground bunkers which may shelter such weapons. The possible use of tactical atomic bombs to implement such aims has, by the way, required a revaluation of the American nuclear doctrine. Nevertheless, it is the interest in WMD shown by terrorist networks such as Al Qaeda[9] and other rogue states which has given preemption absolute priority. As Henry Kissinger said: 'The imminence of proliferation of weapons of mass destruction, the huge dangers it involves, the rejection of a viable inspection system, and the demonstrated hostility of Saddam combine to produce an imperative for preemptive action.'[10]

AIM OF STUDY

The aim of this study is to provide an analysis of facts, with deductions and consequences about the problem of preemption and prevention respectively, and where they stand in the security paradigm. Moreover, it will analyze in depth the legitimacy of such concepts.

OBJECTIVES

The objectives of this book are to:

- *Indicate the links between the definitions of preemption and prevention through a theoretical example.*

- *Identify previous preemptive and preventive actions respectively, by providing historical examples.*

- *Explore legal aspects for waging preemptive and preventive wars.*

- *Analyze the dynamics and challenges of the doctrine of preemption by placing it in the spectrum of preventive measures and conflict.*

- *Assess the importance of intelligence relating to new threats.*

- *Recommend areas for improved action based on the deductions drawn throughout the study.*

SCOPE OF THE STUDY

The study will be limited to the post-Napoleonic era and will focus especially on the war waged by the USA against Iraq in March and April 2003. Additionally, it will focus, in this particular case, on the legal aspects by analyzing in depth the role and the credibility at strategic level of the United Nations' Security Council (UNSC).

REASONS FOR UNDERTAKING THE STUDY

Key Issues in Security Studies Today

At a time when the international community is experimenting with an increasing range of instruments to respond to conflict, developing further understanding of the origins of war, the transformation of strained situations to war and the links needed to improve the role of the United Nations (UN) will be particularly important. UN intervention in recent complex emergencies has resulted in mixed results. The most recent efforts in Iraq, for example, have been fruitless. The UN was not capable of undertaking collective security action, especially after the Iraqi non-compliance with some former UN resolutions in the 1990s. Although UNSC Resolution 1441[11] was accepted on November 8th 2002 by the majority of the permanent members, and thus allocated a team of weapons inspectors led by Dr Hans Blix,[12] the UN failed to achieve a peaceful outcome. Is it because it does not work quickly enough? Is the UN strategic long-term planning in order to avoid war not effective enough? Is it influenced too much by the USA? UN diplomats, US academics and Middle East experts had already warned that the credibility of the UN had been seriously undermined by the US decision that led to the military attack on Iraq.

The proliferation of asymmetric threats, the increasing porosity of borders and the world-wide resonance of conflicts make even rigorous preventive measures perfectible. The traditional defensive shield does not protect anymore. Moreover, strategic complacency or inactivity, which awaits the use of WMD for launching operations in order to stop them, is absolutely irresponsible. Keeping the sword in the scabbard facing a chemical, biological, radiological or nuclear (CBRN) threat subdues states and their population to the permanent blackmail of fanatical organizations. Although deterrence is not dead, it is not effective enough against asymmetric threats. Preemption is therefore a more powerful response to the new threats of the 21st century.

STUDY METHODOLOGY

Preemption is considered as a new doctrine and thus is in vogue. However, too many people, including the media, have too often used it wrongly and sometimes confused it with the notion of prevention. Therefore, it is necessary here to clarify the meaning of these two concepts. In consequence, this study will assess the tangible difference between the definitions of preemption and prevention through a selection of useful dictionaries.

On the other hand, is preemption another face of the changing security paradigm? Some argue that preemption is a new doctrine. The argument that this policy is something completely new is not true. One might say that the new Bush Doctrine is merely a very large extension of the Monroe doctrine.[13] In fact, preemption is nothing new for the USA and has been US policy for a long time. The so often called 'radical' change of the National Security Strategy (NSS) is not so radical indeed. It is revolutionary in its approach, not in its intrinsic concept. It is an adaptation towards new emerging threats, especially such as those of the outrageous attacks of September 11th 2001. People who think preemption is a new US doctrine do not know history and are wrong. One must wonder what the countries throughout Central and South America must think of the Europeans and 'concerned Americans' who are claiming that preemption is something new. Although the USA has not waged preemptive wars yet (there is a controversy about the classification of US led war against Iraq in 2003 [preemptive or preventive]), they could have made preemptive strikes, such as in Guatemala in 1954, Columbia, Bolivia and Peru in the 1960s, Nicaragua in 1981 and Sudan in 1998. Therefore, it is essential to study history and to provide examples which may confirm if they were preemptive or preventive actions. This will be covered in chapter four.

Can such a security paradigm as preemption be applied in relation to international law? Lawyers defending laws, diplomats sticking to the policy of consensus and politicians worried about public opinion often deny this new doctrine. All of these people insist on strictly applying Article 51 of the UNC and on respecting the authority of the UNSC. Thus, they exclude unilateral preemptive actions. The contrary would be surprising, since the specific aim of preemption is to circumvent them. As Henry Kissinger said before the operation in Iraq, 'The new approach is revolutionary. Regime change as a goal for military intervention challenges the international system established by the 1648 Treaty of Westphalia, which after the carnage of the religious wars, established the principle of non-intervention in the domestic affairs of other states. And the notion of justified preemption runs counter to modern international law, which sanctions the use of force in self-defence only against actual, not potential, threats.'[14] Thus, it is worth studying the legitimacy of preemption, particularly the links with the thorny principle of anticipatory self-defence.

If the intent to prevent machinations of asymmetric and fanatical adversaries is not contested, the risks of escalation or precipitation are so high that they imply high rate intelligence. The latter is vital for waging a preemptive war and for convincing the international community about the reality and the imminence of a threat through reliable and believable clues. Therefore, it is worth examining in depth the tasks of the intelligence, especially for asymmetric threats.

Research Methodology

Although the subject of preemption is currently in vogue, the new US NSS and its doctrine of preemption are relatively new, and therefore, there are only a few books up to now dedicated to the approach the author has adopted. Nevertheless, the historical background can be found in several books and articles. The same applies to the legal aspects, especially the principle of anticipatory - or preemptive / preventive - self-defense.

Because the word preemption is fashionable in the mouths of most politicians and the media, a lot of articles and broadcasting have unfortunately used it too often inaccurately. It is thus important to make a clear distinction between the concepts of preemption and prevention, which the majority of articles and speeches do not do.

PRIMARY RESEARCH MATERIAL

Primary research material was reviewed where available in the form of conference attendance and proceedings, journals, reports and evaluations.

SECONDARY RESEARCH MATERIAL

The secondary research material has been taken predominantly from dictionaries, books and Internet sources, and supported with material from journals, serious broadsheets and academic papers. The Beckett and the JSCSC libraries at the Defence Academy of the United Kingdom provided invaluable secondary source material.

There are many recent published articles on the wider issues of international security and they include recent trends in military intervention, which help place the dissertation subject in the broader context of post Cold War conflicts, complex emergencies and the international security architecture.

STUDY STRUCTURE

Chapter One

Chapter one has briefly expounded the imperative for accurately defining the notions of preemption and prevention and giving the reader better insight in the subject. It has also exposed the necessity to refer to historical examples, without which one cannot easily understand exactly what preemption is about. The assessment of the validity of preemption in regard to international law as well as the vital need for irreproachable intelligence has been succinctly developed. Finally, it has outlined the study aim and objectives, its scope as well as its value and the methodology used.

Chapter Two

This chapter focuses on the literature available on this subject. Three main areas are covered. First the historical, second the legal and finally the philosophical literature. It identifies some of the gaps in the available literature and recommends areas and opportunities for improving the knowledge on the subject.

Chapter Three

Chapter three examines the definitions of preemption and prevention and analyzes their links through a theoretical example. It also draws some deductions and considerations for further research.

Chapter Four

This chapter explores previous preemptive respectively preventive actions by providing an historical background. It also draws some personal deductions.

Chapter Five

Chapter five analyses the legitimacy of preemptive and preventive actions and explores the links with the principles of self-defense and anticipatory self-defense.

Chapter Six

This chapter develops arguments about the new calculus of preemption as another face of the changing security paradigm and focuses on the Iraqi case. The importance of intelligence and its challenge regarding the spectrum of new threats are also investigated by providing some personal considerations.

Chapter Seven

The last chapter concludes by presenting a summary of the study. It also identifies gaps and weaknesses as well as strengths and makes appropriate recommendations by providing possible solutions about the conditions for using force.

SPECIAL RECOMMENDATIONS

This book has two purposes. The main is described above in the section entitled 'Objectives.' The second aim is completely different: it is to provide the reader with the opportunity to take a break from the harsh realities discussed in the foregoing chapters. As Professor Christopher Bellamy pointed out in the Foreword he wrote for this book, Napoleon once remarked that 'an Army marches on its stomach.'

It is with this in mind that the author, being both a military officer and an accomplished chef has gone to great lengths to provide the reader with gastronomic recipes that promise to meet those all encompassing human needs: hunger, thirst, and the satisfaction that comes from a good meal.

Therefore, after each chapter the reader will be given or directed to a synergistic part of an entire meal. It is with great pleasure that chapter one begins this journey of knowledge and food with a refreshing non-alcoholic beverage (that way you can keep your wits about you!).

REFRESHING NON-ALCOHOLIC DRINK

Cocktail Salto

Please now turn briefly to the first photograph located in the center of the book. This refreshing non-alcoholic beverage is delightful! If you would like to have the recipe, you are encouraged to visit the website that has been built to accompany Preemptive War located at *www.wonderfood.biz* and of course you are also welcome to visit the author's personal website located at *www.ericklabara.com*.

*"There is unmistakable evidence that
Saddam Hussein is working aggressively to
develop nuclear weapons and will likely have
nuclear weapons within the next five years
... We also should remember we have always
underestimated the progress Saddam has made
in development of weapons of mass destruction."*

Senator Jay Rockefeller (D, WV)
October 10, 2002

CHAPTER TWO
LITERATURE REVIEW

'The man who does not read good books has no advantage over the man who cannot read them.' [15]

Mark Twain (1835-1910)

LITERATURE REVIEW

A t the time of writing this work, to the best of the author's knowledge, there were no books available that specifically addressed preemption. There were many books that dealt with prevention in its broad meaning, usually in the form of 'conflict prevention' and more in a diplomatic than a military sense. Several other books mention the issue of preemptive war in some of their chapters and paragraphs, especially in the historical, legal and philosophical literature. On the other hand, scores of articles in journals and newspapers were available about this subject, as well as on the Internet. An Internet search conducted with the research engine 'Google'[16] on April 10th 2004 yielded 191,000 entries by selecting 'preemptive war' and 197,000 entries using 'preemptive war + preemptive'. Thus, this chapter covers the literature that was available to the author on this subject at the time in these three main areas and explores the gaps which have been addressed throughout this book. That being said, it is not the intent of the author to list all the literature which has been read regarding this subject, but rather to provide you – the reader – with a general overview of the collected sources. The notes and bibliography should offer the reader enough material to assess the validity of the literature in this study.

HISTORICAL LITERATURE

Several books have been read about alleged preventive or preemptive wars. Most of them describe quite deeply the conflicts and battles themselves and explore as well their roots. However, the author had to read between the lines because most books did not rely specifically on preemption or prevention.

Articles in specialized journals and newspapers were probably the best source to tackle the problem of preemption and prevention. Moreover, the Internet has been also a good source, albeit this source is not always reliable. Though the subject is quite new, scores of interesting literature has been examined in order to extract the quintessence of the studied subject.

LEGAL LITERATURE

Several books refer to the problem of the use of force in the realm of international law. These also examine the thorny problem of anticipatory self-defense which is obviously narrowly linked to preemption and prevention. Because almost all serious books more or less say the same things on the subject, only a few have been chosen for this study.

Recent articles in specialized journals describing the legitimacy of the war against Iraq in 2003 have been taken for references. The Internet has been also a valuable source of information, though great care and attention has been needed in selecting qualitative relevant literature.

PHILISOPHICAL LITERATURE

State moralist position and moral justification of war or military intervention in the absence of covert aggression are the subjects of most books relating to preemptive and preventive actions. Ethics and morality on this issue are illustrated in several books which has enabled the author to acquire a general overview on this subject. However, some books have biased opinions and the author's impartiality has contributed to the rejection of some ideas. On the other hand, the concept of prevention and preemption are often intertwined and a lot of literature does not distinguish between the subtleties of the two notions, which prompted the author to examine their true definitions in serious dictionaries.

Scores of articles and reports in journals and newspapers have been explored about this subject. Although mixed impressions have crossed the author's mind, valuable literature has been found on the subject. Official reports have been also explored, such as US and British documents relating to the latest conflict in Iraq.

Deductions

The reading of these types of literature has guided the author to consider the gaps which had to be identified, then select and eventually analyze them. This process led the author to analyze the facts discovered in the literature and to draw relevant deductions and consequences on:

- *the definitions of the notions of preemption and prevention;*

- *historical references;*

- *the legitimacy of the concepts of preemption and prevention;*

- *the place of these concepts in the security paradigm.*

THE FIRST ENTRÉE

Soupe Mulligatawny

Traditionally, the soup comes first in a seven course meal. This delectable offering is called Mulligatawny Soup and originates from India. It is a wonderful curry chicken with savory onions, curcuma, zesty lemon, and smooth coconut milk.

Please now turn briefly to the second photograph located in the center of the book. Remember also that these recipes and more can be found at *www.wonderfood.biz* and of course my own website *www.ericklabara.com*.

"There is no doubt that ... Saddam Hussein has invigorated his weapons programs. Reports indicate that biological, chemical and nuclear programs continue apace and may be back to pre-Gulf War status. In addition, Saddam continues to redefine delivery systems and is doubtless using the cover of a licit missile program to develop longer-range missiles that will threaten the United States and our allies."

from a letter to President Bush signed by
Senator Bob Graham (D, FL)
December 5, 2001

CHAPTER THREE
PREEMPTION OR PREVENTION?

*'The greatest enemy of knowledge is not the igno-
rance of knowledge but the illusion of it.'[17]*

Stephen Hawking (1942 -)

DEFINITIONS

For further understanding, it is now necessary to investigate the meaning of the concepts of 'preemption' and 'prevention'. The research for a definition of both terms has been done using several dictionaries, four of which have been relevant: first, the *Webster's Ninth New Collegiate Dictionary*, second the *Cobuild English Dictionary for Advanced Learners*, third the *New Shorter Oxford English Dictionary on Historical Principles* and finally the US Department of Defense's own official Dictionary of Military Terms.

The word preempt finds its roots in the Latin *'prae'* (before) and *'emptus'*, the latter being the past participle of the verb *'emere'*, which means 'to buy', literally, 'the action to buy before'. In the figurative meaning, the *Webster's Ninth New Collegiate Dictionary* defines preemptive (preemption) as 'a prior seizure or appropriation, a taking [of] possession before others'[18] and preemption as an action 'marked by the seizing of the initiative'[19] in other words, 'initiated by oneself'. On the other hand, the *Cobuild English Dictionary for Advanced Learners* gives the following definitions of preemption: an action is preempted if one 'prevents it from happening by doing something which makes it unnecessary or impossible.'[20] A preemptive attack or strike therefore is 'intended to weaken or damage an enemy or opponent, for example, by destroying their weapons before they can do any harm.'[21]

Both dictionaries give satisfactory definitions of the intrinsic meaning of the words 'preemption' and 'preemptive' but they are not clear enough about the immediacy of an enemy's or opponent's hostile action. However, the *New Shorter Oxford English Dictionary on Historical Principles* is more precise about this subject; to preempt is defined as 'to prevent (an occurrence) or stop (a person) by anticipatory action' whereas preemption is described as 'the action or strategy of making a preemptive attack.'[22] Preemptive action thus is defined as 'intended to forestall an enemy who is thought to be about to attack.'[23] Here the notion of immediacy is better depicted as in the first two dictionaries. Moreover, the *US Department of Defense's Dictionary on Military Terms* defines preemption very accurately as 'an attack initiated on the basis of incontrovertible evidence that an enemy attack is imminent.'[24] Therefore, it can be deduced that the word preemption and the meaning of a preemptive attack or strike respectively, must include not only the notion of anticipation but also the one of imminence of a danger or a threat.

'Prevention' and 'preventive action' are slightly different concepts to preemption and preemptive action. The root of the verb 'prevent' is also Latin. *'Prae'* added with *'venire'* means literally 'to come before' and figuratively 'to anticipate, to forestall [...] to keep from happening or existing'[25], 'to deprive of power or hope of acting or succeeding'[26], 'to ensure that something does not happen'[27], and 'to forestall or thwart by previous or precautionary measures.'[28] The first dictionary describes the word preventive as 'undertaken to forestall anticipated hostile action'[29] whereas the second one defines it as 'intended to help prevent things such as diseases or crime.'[30] The third dictionary gives nearly the same definitions. Prevention is described as 'the action of stopping something from happening or making impossible an anticipated event or intended act [...] Action intended to provide against an anticipated danger'[31] whereas preventive as 'that anticipates in order to preclude; that stops something from happening; that acts as a hindrance or obstacle.'[32] The fourth dictionary is however more accurate as it defines preventive war as 'initiated in the belief that military conflict, while not imminent, is inevitable, and that to delay would involve greater risk.'[33]

THEORETICAL EXAMPLE

The subsequent example from Lawrence Freedman, Professor of War Studies at Kings College in London, might enlighten the reader about these concepts.[34] Assuming that country A is in conflict with country B, A is confident that it has deterred B because of its determination to defend its vital and national interests. Deterrence works because B cannot foresee any prospect of substantial gains: it would face either tough resistance (denial) or retaliation (punishment) from A.

'A Preventive war occurs when statesmen believe merely that war is better now than later.'[35] Considering that B does not comply with international agreements, for example, breach of international treaties or of United Nations' resolutions, B might get stronger and, in the eyes of A, could successfully fight deterrence by dulling the impact of retaliation. Moreover, if diplomatic efforts have failed and economic sanctions not been effective enough, A might decide to prevent B from reaching this position by waging a preventive war. Although the threat posed by B is not imminent, but indeed could imperil international peace and security in the medium term (two to four years), A will try to disarm B, in order to keep it militarily inferior. A will probably also like to change B's political status, in order to reduce the potential threat posed by B's government. 'Prevention exploits existing strategic advantages by depriving another state of the capacity to pose a threat and/ or eliminating the state's motivation to pose a threat through regime change.'[36] Consequently, prevention provides a means of combating the development of a threat before it has had the chance to become imminent.

Prevention, however, does not only mean war, but refers to a repertoire of strategies to forestall a threat through a variety of means, including in extreme circumstances, the possible use of force. Thus, prevention includes the panoply of non-military preventive instruments that can be used to avoid the development of a threat. Such instruments will be developed in chapter six.

Should A decide not to wage a preventive war against B and the latter strengthen its power through additional lethal capacity, B might consider that it has acquired the necessary means to safely take initiative against A. Besides having regrets not to have taken some sort of action before, A might judge the situation as extremely urgent and wage a preemptive war against B.

'A preemptive war takes place at some point between the moment when an enemy decides to attack - or, more precisely, is perceived to be about to attack - and when the attack is actually launched.'[37]

This is where there might be a legitimate justification for anticipatory self-defense under Article 51 of the United Nation's Charter (UNC). As the 'perception of the threat derives from the interaction of capabilities with intentions'[38] ($T = C \times I$), the challenges for A are to analyze the evidence of an imminent

Strength	A >> B (B weak)	A > B (B getting stronger)	A ≥ B (B getting much stronger)
Previous Measures	Possible diplomatic and/or economic sanctions	• B capable to fight A's deterrence; • Diplomatic and/or economic sanctions failed or not effective enough to reduce the threat	• B capable to fight A's deterrence and A's preventive measures; • Diplomatic and/or economic sanctions failed
Threat	Could become hostile but threat perceived as poor	Hostile but not imminent	Hostile and imminent
Strategy	**Deterrence**	**Preventive war**	**Preemptive war**

Table 1: Deterrence, Preventive and Preemptive Wars
Source: Author

attack by quantifying B's capability, qualifying B's intentions and finally assessing the ability of its own forces to disrupt the attack.

Sir Lawrence Freedman's analysis of this question was simultaneously and quite independently duplicated by the author, who has further developed Professor Freedman's concepts in table 1.

DEDUCTIONS

It can be deduced that both preemption and prevention can be considered as anticipatory controlling strategies in order to counter enemies who do not make cautious decisions at national and international policy levels. These strategies assume that, given the circumstances, an enemy might use force and therefore cannot be allowed to pose a threat to its direct neighbors as well as to endanger international peace and security. In contrast, 'coercive strategies such as deterrence assume that an adversary's relevant calculations can be influenced.'[39]

Preemptive war is then justified by an imminent and real threat of attack, a clear present danger that a threatening country is about to attack another country and is a danger to international security. In such a case a preemptive attack is recognized as justifiable. Preventive war, on the other hand, is not well received by the international community because the threat is not imminent and is too vague or not tangible enough to be recognized as a threat. It may be a potential future threat but this can be dealt with by other means than the use of force. Indeed, it is essential to distinguish between the objective existence of an imminent threat of an attack, its true perception and its use as a pretext for starting military operations. Paradoxically, preemptive is a natural reflex against a well-defined imminent threat whereas prevention has a much more aggressive character. Therefore, preventive wars are considered unlawful. This aspect will be covered in chapter five.

Imminence: a concept to be reconsidered

If preemptive wars may be better received than preventive ones, another problem arises from the notion of imminence. Imminence is defined as 'something which is 'almost certain to happen very soon.'[40] 'Almost certain' is for some not certain enough and therefore the concept of imminence need to be reconsidered. The difficulty is to assess the immediacy of the threat by evaluating the intent of a potential adversary. The desire to thwart the emergence of a threat with such characteristic 'helps to explain the argument, found in the US NSS, the concept of imminence, upon which the grounds for preemption are based, needs to be reconsidered.'[41]

In order to clearly distinguish between preemption and prevention, the subsequent chapter will analyze twelve selected historical cases, going from the first inter-nationally recognized preemptive strike by British forces which occurred in the USA in December 1837; to the latest US led Gulf War[42] in March - April 2003 against Iraq.

THE SECOND ENTRÉE

Carpaccio de saumon au poivre rose

This finely sliced salmon with pink pepper is a phenomenal dish that is served cold. The salmon's rich texture and brilliant color make it a natural for showing off; your senses will be overwhelmed.

Please now turn briefly to the third photograph located in the center of the book. Remember also that these recipes and more can be found at *www.wonderfood.biz* and of course my own website *www.ericklabara.com*.

"*We begin with the common belief that Saddam Hussein is a tyrant and a threat to the peace and stability of the region. He has ignored the mandated of the United Nations and is building weapons of mass destruction and the means of delivering them.*"

Senator Carl Levin (D, MI)
September 19, 2002

CHAPTER FOUR
HISTORICAL BACKGROUND

'Experience is a lantern which lights the traveled path.'[43]

Confucius (551-479 BC)

THE CAROLINE CASE (1837)[44]

During the insurrection in Canada in 1837, unrest occurred at various places in the United States, especially
along the Canadian border. The Government of the USA adopted active measures for the enforcement of the neutrality
laws, but the difficulties of the situation were increased by the
course of the insurgents, who, when defeated, sought refuge in
the United States, where they endeavored to recruit their forces. The rebel leaders, despite steps taken by the USA to prevent
a private militia being formed, managed in December 1837, to
enlist at Buffalo in the USA the support of a large number of
American nationals. The resulting Canadian rebellion force,
established on Navy Island in Canadian waters, attacked passing British ships. This force was supplied from the USA's shore
by an American ship named "Caroline",[45] which transported
arms and men. The British responded with a night raid on the
night of December 29th by capturing the vessel as it was docked
at Fort Schlosser, New York, setting it on fire and sending it
over Niagara Falls.

British forces in Canada used preemptive attack on the 'Caroline', manned by these Canadian rebels who were planning attacks from the USA. In this particular case, preemptive action
was used because of a well-defined and imminent threat.

THE ANGLO-ZULU WAR (1879)

The Anglo-Zulu War of 1879 remains one of the most dramatic
in both British and southern African history. The aim of this
paragraph is to assess if it was a preemptive or preventive war,
which was provoked by an act of British aggression. The Zulu

kingdom had first emerged early in the nineteenth century, with its heartland lying along the eastern seaboard of southern Africa, north of the town of Port Natal, called today Durban. In 1824 and within a few years, 'the first white adventurers sailed into the Bay of Port Natal - now Durban - lured by tales of clusters of huts ringed with palisades of ivory'[46] and were attracted to Zululand in search of trade, hunt and profit. In 1838, the Boers entered the province of Natal. This arrival worried the British authorities in Cape Town, 'who took immediate steps to isolate Port Natal, to prevent them from reaching the sea and thereby opening contact with rival European powers.'[47] In 1842 after a severe fight at the Port, the Boers withdrew and Natal became a British colony on the southern borders of Zululand.

By the 1870s, the British began to adopt a new policy in the region, hoping to bring the various British colonies, Boer republics (such as Transvaal) and independent African groups under a single British authority, in the aim to implement a policy of economic development. This 'forward policy' was Confederation. In 1877, 'using the pretext that the Transvaal Republic was bankrupt and unable to defend itself against its African enemies, Britain stepped in and annexed it.'[48] At the same time, a new British representative, Sir Henry Bartle Edward Frere (1815 - 1884) was sent to the Cape with the clear intention to implement the new Confederation policy. He became the British High Commissioner in South Africa.

Sir Henry Bartle Frere believed that the robust and economically independent Zulu kingdom was a threat to this policy. It is true that the very charismatic King Shaka (1778 - 1828) who had perhaps 400 warriors in 1816 was able to grow the kingdom to have as many as 15,000 by the time of his death.[49] Further, King Cetshwayo (1827 - 1884) was able to successfully expand Zulu territory from its original modest size to one which was substantially larger by 1870.[50] This may indeed have been a major concern for Frere.

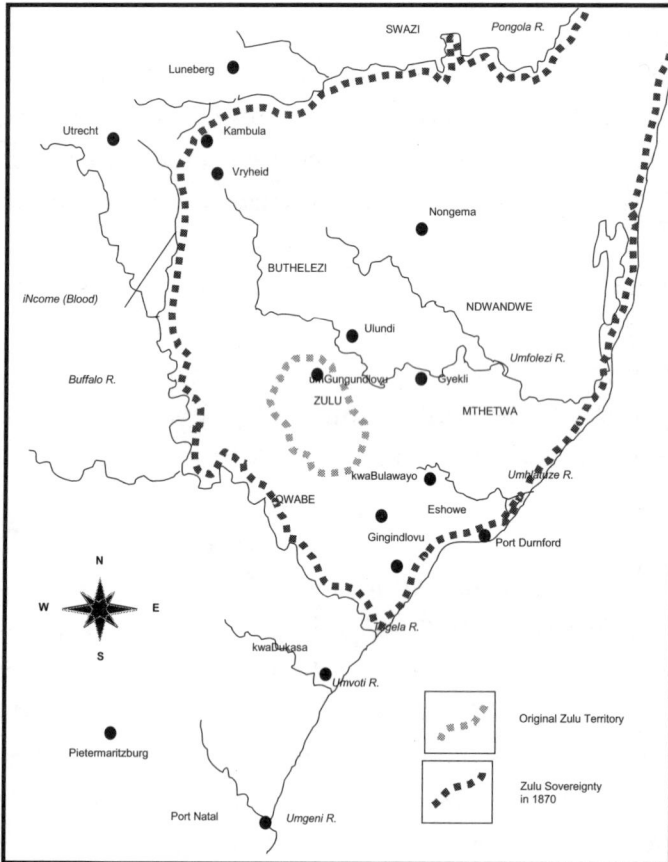

Map 1: Expansion of the Zulu Territory
Source: Angus McBride, The Zulu War, (Osprey Publishing Ltd., London, 1976), p. 3. Graphic by the author

It was said that King Cetshwayo's army was as large as 50,000 men strong[51] and known as 'probably the most mobile foot-soldiers in the world.'[52] It is nevertheless worth asking if these were a real and imminent or only a potential future threat to the British Colony of Natal. The reality is that King Cetshewayo was not threatening to attack Natal and was in fact on good terms with the British until the end of 1878.

Anyway, Sir Henry Bartle Frere was convinced that 'the biggest obstacle to Confederation was the independent Zulu kingdom.'[53] Therefore, he wanted the power of the Zulu king broken, so that other black groups would see no hope in resistance and thus, be forced to admit the advantages of the Confederation. In 1878, Frere was looking for a reason to provoke a confrontation and he found one. 'An important Zulu border chieftain, Shihayo kaXongo, crossed into Natal in pursuit of two of the chief's runaway wives.'[54] The women were captured by his sons, brought back into Zululand and put to death. Frere asked Cetshewayo to surrender the perpetrators but the Zulu king did not comply.

In December 1878 he picked a quarrel with the Zulu king in the belief that the Zulu army, armed primarily with shields and spears, would soon collapse in the face of British Imperial might. Moreover, at the surprise of the Zulu, the British presented an ultimatum on December 11th 1878: they were required not only to surrender Shihayo's sons, but also disband their army. Cetshwayo could obviously not accede to these demands. The war began in January 1879 with the invasion of Zululand by three columns of British troops under the command of Lt. Gen. Lord Chelmsford.

It can be deduced, that the British Imperial administration in the Cape colony in Southern Africa saw the Zulu kingdom as a challenge to their authority and in order to contain this perceived threat, they engineered a war. It is questionable however to have assessed the Zulus as a threat for Natal. According to the definitions mentioned in the last chapter, it can be concluded that this was not a preemptive but a preventive war, as king Cetshewayo did not imminently threat to attack the British colony and experienced friendly relationships with them until the end of 1878. Thus, this preventive war can be considered as an unwarranted act of British aggression.

PEARL HARBOR (DECEMBER 7, 1941)

In 1941, after the formation of the Wang Tsing-Wie government in Nankin in the province of Kiang Sou, Japanese influence expanded in the South of China with the invasion of the Chinese provinces of Kouang Si and Kouang Toung[55] consolidating their position with the occupation of French Indochina in July 1941. Tchang Kai-Chek's China was suddenly isolated and this situation threatened the dispatching of raw material sources from Malaysia and Indonesia. As a consequence, the USA imposed an oil and scrap embargo on Japan, which weakened Japanese rearmament. On the 7th December 1941, Japanese forces attacked Pearl Harbor as retaliation, action which can be considered as a preemptive strike against the USA in order to defeat US based troops in the Pacific before other US sanctions could be imposed.

ISRAEL'S SIX DAY WAR (JUNE 5-10, 1967)

The Egyptians, as well as other Arab nations, believed that 'the founding of Israel in 1948 had been unjust, that the state had no rightful existence, and hence that it could be attacked at any time.'[56] On May 14th 1967, the Egyptian government put its armed forces on 'maximum alert' and began a major build-up of its troops in the Sinai, and then, on May 22nd blocked the Straits of Tiran to passage by Israeli vessels. Moreover, the Egyptian president Nasser made a major speech on May 29th announcing that if war came, the goal would be nothing less than the destruction of Israel. Moreover, he concluded an alliance with Jordan's King Hussein on May 30th placing the Jordanian army under Egyptian command in event of war. Syria had already agreed to such an agreement and on June 4th, Iraq joined the alliance. After some debates in the Israeli cabinet as to whether to not to wage war, a strike on June 5th 1967 against Egypt, Jordan and Syria, but did not seek to rely specifically on preemption or anticipatory self defense. Nevertheless, Israel, through a spectacular and lightning offensive, counterattacked in conquering the right bank of the Jordan River, including the Golan Heights, and the old town of Jerusalem. Almost at the same time, Israel attacked Egyptian forces in the Sinai Peninsula and repelled them relatively quickly. Because of the emergence and the imminence of the threat, Israel did need to take military initiative to secure victory. Thus, this war was definitely preemptive. Afterwards, Israel alleged that the blocking of the Straits of Tiran was an act of war and that the major build-up of Egyptian forces represented a sufficient and imminent threat justifying self defense under Article 51 of the UNC. However, 'some states rejected this claim and ruled out the legality of anticipatory use of force,'[57] in other words, preemption.

South Africa Against Nambia and Neighbors

The UN had been concerned about Namibia since 1948, when South Africa first purported to incorporate the mandated territory. In 1966, the UN General Assembly terminated the

South African mandate over Namibia and placed it under the responsibility of the UN, but South Africa continued illegally to occupy Namibia. In fact, South Africa illegally occupied front-line parts of Namibia, and other neighboring states such as Angola, Botswana, Mozambique and Zambia, invoking anticipatory self defense and preemptive action against incursions by guerrilla fighters and terrorists seeking the liberation of these states. South Africa justified its invasion by pretending that these states had been supporting terrorist actions by allowing the use of their territory for organizations like the African National Congress (ANC) and the South West Africa People's organization (SWAPO). South Africa relied however on the new doctrine of 'hot pursuit'. 'This is a law of sea doctrine whereby coastal states have the right to pursue ships guilty of offences in territorial waters into areas of the sea beyond national jurisdiction.'[58] This tactic is described in the Convention on the Law of the Sea of 1982, in Article 111.[59] By analogy, South Africa claimed the right to pursue presumed guerrilla fighters and terrorists into neighboring states considering that these were a sufficient and immediate threat to South African integrity and sovereignty. South African claims and the doctrine of 'hot pursuit' were of course rejected by the ICJ with the UN Resolution 568 (1985) which condemned the South African incursions in Namibia and other neighboring states. This invoked the breach of Article 2(4) of the UNC and Article 60(3) of the Vienna Convention on the Law of Treaties of 1969[60] (see also chapter 5).

USA AGAINST NICARAGUA (1981)

When the American military forces left Nicaragua for the last time, in 1933, they left behind a souvenir by which the Nicaraguan people could remember them: the National Guard, placed under the direction of one Anastasio Somoza. Three years later, Somoza took over the presidency and with the indispensable help of the National Guard established a family dynasty which would rule over Nicaragua, much like a private estate, for the next 43 years. However, in 1979, 'the right-wing Somoza government was overthrown by revolution by the left-winged Sandinista government.'[61] In 1981, President Reagan decided to stop economic aid to Nicaragua, accusing the Sandinista government of aiding guerrillas fighting against the El Salvador government, which was on good terms with the USA, by allowing Soviet weaponry to pass through its ports and territory en route for El Salvador. In consequence, the USA laid mines in Nicaraguan territorial waters and attacked naval bases and oil installations. It is true, that during the Cold War period, the USA fought communism with determination. In the eyes of the Reagan administration, the intervention in Nicaragua was justified by the imminent threat of the destabilization of a whole region by sympathizers of Marxist insurrection. The USA did not want to have another communist block in the backyard. Preemptive incursions were therefore performed in order to stop such dangerous expansion.

OTHER STRUGGLES IN LATIN AMERICA

Nicaragua was not the only example in Central and South America. The worst case was Guatemala in 1954, totally unjustified by any real threat of Soviet intervention there. In this case, conservatives using the Black Legend[62] thought they could support the militaries, under the praetorian concept already discussed, and block out communist activity. In 1961 came the Kennedy doctrine of counter-insurgency, humane and totally compatible with the Just War theory[63] as a system of internal defense. The doctrines were effective in Colombia, Bolivia, and Peru, to name a few examples. But in the 1970s, ugly civil wars on the South American continent opposed communist terrorists against state sponsored terrorism in the name of anticommunist, counter-insurgency doctrine, in reality a French Algerian concept that freely advocated the preemptive killing of citizens identified with the radical left.

ISRAEL AGAINST IRAQ (1981)

Menachem Begin, then Prime Minister of Israel, faced the same dilemma in June 1981 that Iran had faced with Saddam Hussein's Iraq. For two years the Israelis had watched apprehensively as Saddam appeared to be close to using nuclear weapons. The centerpiece of his effort was a French-built Osirak-type nuclear reactor turning out plutonium at Tuwaitah. 'Begin viewed Saddam as a latter-day Hitler and, continuing the analogy, Saddam's nuclear program as the potential instrument of a new Final Solution against the Jewish state.'[64]

Under no circumstances would Israel allow an enemy to develop WMD against it. This analysis and the assessment of the Mossad, the Israeli intelligence services, that the nuclear reactor was on the verge of becoming operational, drove Israel's decision to conduct an air strike. After considerable internal debate within the Israeli ruling circle, Begin ordered his aircraft to bomb it on June 7th in order to derail the Iraqi nuclear bomb effort. Israel invoked preemption and anticipatory self-defense.

The Israeli action was unanimously condemned by the Security Council as "'a clear violation" of Article 2(4)'[65] of the UNC. Could the threat posed by the nuclear reactor in Tuwaitah have been regarded as sufficiently imminent for the purposes of any right of preemptive action? In fact, this air strike is an instance of prevention rather than preemption, as an Iraqi concrete use of a weapon was not imminent.

USA AGAINST SUDAN (1998)

The most extensive use of preventive strikes, by states invoking Article 51 of the UNC but in reality going far beyond the bounds of its provisions, has been by the USA and Israel in response to terrorist attacks on nationals abroad. They were taken by Israel in 1968 against Lebanon and in 1985 against Tunisia, and by the USA against Libya in 1986, Iraq in 1983, Sudan in 1998 and Afghanistan in 1998 and 2002. In all these cases, force was used in response to past terrorist attacks against the state allegedly harboring the terrorist organization responsible.

Let us examine the case of the US strike against a pharmaceutical plant located in Khartoum, Sudan. On August 20th 1998, in response to terrorist attacks on US embassies in Kenya and Ethiopia in August 1998, 'US cruise missiles destroyed the al-Shifa pharmaceutical plant in Khartoum, Sudan, which the Clinton administration charged was linked to the terrorist, Osama bin Laden, and was producing a precursor chemical for VX nerve gas.'[66] The Clinton administration alleged that the pharmaceutical plant produced chemical weapons for terrorist activities. According to Bill Clinton, former President of the USA, 'these preventive strikes were a necessary and proportionate response to the imminent threat of further terrorist attacks.'[67]

The USA invoked the right of self-defense under Chapter VII, Article 51 of the UNC. Nevertheless, these strikes, called preventive by former President Bill Clinton were indeed preemptive, because of the imminence of the threat and the actual danger posed by this plant and its links with terrorist organizations.

9/11 and the USA Against Afghanistan (2001)

The fall of the Berlin Wall in 1989 was a symbolic event which raised hopes for a more united world, founded on the values of international legality and democracy. The idea was put forward that, at last, human rights would be respected planet-wide and violent conflict would gradually disappear. In just over a decade, many such hopes have been replaced by power politics or *Realpolitik*,[68] especially after the horrendous events of September 11th 2001 (often referred as 9/11). As a symbol of an historical turnaround, the terrorist destruction of the Twin Towers of the New York City's World Trade Centre (WTC) and of the Pentagon in Arlington, Virginia has abruptly put an end to the twelve-years-holiday of history. These absolutely gratuitous terrorist attacks in the USA have changed the course of history because for the first time ever, the super-power had been hit and had shown its vulnerability.

As the smoke cleared away from the ruins of the WTC, government investigation identified with increasing confidence that Al Qaeda, a terrorist enterprise led by Osama Bin Laden, linked with a fundamentalist regime known as the Taliban in Afghanistan, carried the responsibility for that outrage and for a chain of terrorist atrocities directed against the USA. This raised the profile of international global terrorism. Politicians and the media employed the terms of 'global conspiracy' justifying a forceful response from a universal coalition.[69]

The horrendous attacks of September 11th can be considered as a preemptive attack against the USA because, in the view of Al-Qaeda's terrorist group, America is a permanent and immediate threat to the world. Indeed, one of the goals of Al Qaeda and its terrorist branches is 'the destruction of the United States of America.'[70]

Nevertheless, these attacks were hardly decisive and 'it was possible to deal with the perpetrators in an effort to ensure that such a blow would never be struck again.'[71] President Bush launched the first offensive in the war on terrorism on September 23rd by signing an Executive Order freezing the US-based assets of individuals and organizations involved with terrorism. The US response continued with a military campaign against the Taliban Regime in Afghanistan, in the operation called 'Enduring Freedom' which began on October 7th 2001. Since then, coalition forces have liberated the Afghan people from the repressive and violent Taliban regime, without being sure yet about the fate of Al-Qaeda's leader, Osama Bin Laden.

This war against a regime supporting the Al-Qaeda terrorist network was the response to the September 11th attacks. It could also be considered as preventive, to the extent that the Taliban regime posed a real threat, however not an imminent one, to international peace and security by harboring one of the deadliest terrorist sub-states organization. The doctrine of preemption is a prudent and effective approach to the war on terrorism, as 'it provides sound guidance for dealing with security problems within and arising from weak states. But again, prevention is more applicable in this context rather than preemptive - acting early rather than late, while a problem gestates but before it erupts, using all available means.'[72] Given the circumstances, quick response and preemptive strikes will of course be the adequate manner in which to tackle the imminence of a terrorist attack, 'but deterrence is not necessarily impossible under such circumstances,[73] such as public warnings.

GULF WAR III[74] (2003)

What about the situation between the USA and Iraq? As mentioned above, the USA has sometimes used force in preemptive actions or strikes but has never undertaken a preemptive war in all of its history. Some would argue that the invasion of Panama[75] that led to the capture of Manuel Noriega was preventive rather than preemptive. Nevertheless, an important question has to be posed here: why has the USA waged a preventive / preemptive war against Iraq?

Improving security and advancing a political settlement in Israel and Palestine is essential to the USA's 'two central post-11 September foreign policy pillars: counter-terrorism and counter-proliferation of weapons of mass destruction.'[76] Iraq's regime posed a clear threat to its Arab neighbors as well as to the US and its allies. First of all, there was the fear of the Iraqi development of WMD (see Appendices A1-A5) and second, the only way for the Bush administration to be certain of removing WMD from Iraq was to remove Saddam Hussein's regime from power. Given Saddam Hussein's long history of terror, the US and its allies could not allow such a dangerous regime to acquire the most lethal weapons. Saddam Hussein has never lived up to his obligations to disclose WMD and destroy them. Thus, Washington should not have allowed him to continue to make a charade of those obligations as he did in the aftermath of the 1991 Gulf war. Because the Security Council defaulted on its obligation to enforce its own resolutions, particularly UN Resolution 1441, the US had to disarm Iraq by the use of force. The UN was not capable of undertaking collective security action, so that the US was fully within its rights to defend its own national interests by waging a war. Moreover, if Iraq's WMD development program had not been blocked, it would have been 'all the more difficult to constrain Iranian nuclear ambitions.'[77] Other countries complained about US 'unilateralism', but it is worth stressing that the Bush administration has bent over backwards to include the Security Council.

Another important deduction based on historical facts is what the Bush administration was discussing in terms of Iraq, was an imminent and real threat of attack on the USA, Israel or even on any of Iraq's neighbors, which might justify a preemptive strike. Was it indeed an imminent threat? Some argue that there was no imminent threat and that the Bush administration attacked Iraq to prevent or neutralize a potential future threat. Preemption as a strategic concept has been introduced in connection with the dangers posed by WMD. 'Preemption pertains narrowly to military action when actual WMD use by an adversary is imminent.[78] However 'prevention refers to a repertoire of strategies to forestall the acquisition of WMD through a variety of means, including, in extreme circumstances, the possible use of force.'[79]

Saddam Hussein had a calculating nature, in addition to an extreme ruthlessness, and an indubitable fascination for all types of destructive instruments. The current problem is that only few or insignificant WMD has been found. The smoking gun has not been discovered yet. Nevertheless, 'Iraq, by the best

Conflicts / Types of conflicts	Preemptive strike	Preemptive war	Preventive strike	Preventive war
Caroline case (1837)	x			
Zulu war (1879)				x
Pearl Harbor (1941)	x			
Six Days War (1967)		x		
Namibia (1966-70)	x			
Latin America (1970s)	x		(x)	
Nicaragua (1981)	x		(x)	
Iraq (Osirak, 1981)			x	
Sudan (1998)	x			
September 11th 2001	x			
Afghanistan (2001)				x
Iraq (2003)				x

Table 2: Conflicts and Types of Conflicts
Source: Author

available evidence, did not have the capability or any immediate intention to attack its neighbors or the US with chemical, biological or nuclear weapons.'[80] This is one of the reasons why the 2003 war against Iraq was not a preemptive war but rather a preventive one.

As well as this, although Saddam had a long history involved with terror, there is still no evidence that he had links with Osama Bin Laden. An argument for action before he had done so would have been preventive rather then preemptive. Neither the US agenda, nor possible proliferation of rogue states required the placing of the doctrine of preemption at the centre of the NSS. 'Precisely because of their military superiority, the USA and its allies did not need to take military initiative to secure victory. Instead, military operations were geared towards containing conflicts – mitigating their effects, coercing guilty parties, and establishing law and order.'[81]

In this case of the 2003 Iraq war, the USA had attacked Iraqi assets and overthrown Saddam's regime before imminent dangers had had a chance to emerge. Thus it can be concluded that this war was definitively preventive and not preemptive, as the language in vogue has too often and wrongly suggested.

SUMMARY

With the few examples mentioned above, it can be shown that most of these were preemptive / preventive actions or strikes and not specifically preemptive wars, except for the 1967 Israel's victorious Six Day War which constitutes 'the only unambiguously clear case of preemptive war in the post-Napoleonic era.'[82] Table 2 summarizes what has been covered in this chapter.

MAIN COURSE

Carré d'agneau à la Provençale

The Provencal-Style Rack of Lamb with young spring Thyme is an incredible dish that serves as a fantastic main course for those who love tender grilled meat. However, for vegetarians, the next dish after chapter five would be more suited to your pallet.

Please now turn briefly to the fourth photograph located in the center of the book. Remember also that these recipes and more can be found at *www.wonderfood.biz* and of course my own website *www.ericklabara.com*.

© Copyright Alain Besson. Used with permission.
http://www.wonderfood.biz

1. Cocktail Salto

2. Soupe Mulligatawny

3. Carpaccio de saumon au poivre rose

4. Carré d'agneau à la Provençale

5. Wok Végétarien

6. Plateau de fromages

7. Salade d'oranges

"War is an ugly thing, but not the ugliest of things. The decayed and degradaded state of moral and patriotic feeling which thinks that nothing is worth war is much worse. The person who has nothing for which he is willing to fight, nothing which is more important than his own personal safety, is a miserable creature and has no chance of being free unless made and kept so by the exertions of better men than himself."

John Stuart Mill

CHAPTER FIVE
LEGAL ASPECTS

'Peace is not sought in order to provide war, but war is waged in order to attain peace.' [83]

St Augustine of Hippo (354 - 430 AD)

LEGAL ASPECTS

E very use of force which is not authorized by the UNC and which is contrary to the goals of the UN is incompatible with international law. Article 2(4) of the UNC provides a general prohibition of the threat or the use of force. It is worth quoting:

'All Members shall refrain in their international relations from the threat or the use of force against the territorial integrity or political independence of any state, or in any other manner inconsistent with the Purposes of the United Nations.'[84]

However, there are exceptions to that principle:

First, coercive measures by the Security Council (SC) or coercive actions dictated and authorized by the SC and executed by a nominated state, which means that the use of force can be realized. This system is foreseen in Chapter VII, Articles 43 and 47 of the UNC, but has seldom been activated in the history of the UN, essentially because of the Cold War. Valuable examples are provided by Steve Haines in a contribution on military interventions used in the realm of international law.[85]

Secondly, the law of self defense or legitimate defense has been the 'subject of the most fundamental disagreements between states and between writers.'[86] Nevertheless, the right of self defense is clearly mentioned in Article 5 of the North Atlantic Treaty Organization[87] (NATO) and in the Chapter VII, Article 51 of the UNC. In order to understand the latter article, it seems appropriate now to reveal its contents:

'Nothing in the present Charter shall impair the inherent right of individual or collective self defense if an armed attack occurs against a Member of the United Nations, until the Security Council has taken measures necessary to maintain international peace and security. Measures taken by Members in the exercise of this right of self defense shall be immediately reported to the Security Council and shall not in any way affect the authority and responsibility of the Security Council under the present Charter to take at any time such action as it deems necessary in order to maintain or restore international peace and security.'[88]

Article 51 of the UNC refers to the natural customary right of legitimate defense, namely a legal use of force foreseen by international law. The question is to know in which situations it is permitted to use force as self defense. Article 51 of the UNC uses the term 'armed attack,'[89] so that not every use of force allows self defense.

Individual and collective self defense

The aim of this study is not to develop the diverse sorts of self defense. However, it seems appropriate here to provide some explanations about the different kinds of this customary right. The exercise of the right of self defense can be individual or collective. Individual self defense obviously concerns the right of self defense of a state against another attacking state. Collective self defense means that if a state is the victim of an armed attack, other states can supply aid, but only providing that the attacked state has recognized it is the victim of an armed attack and has asked for assistance from a third party. Further considerations can be consulted in the specialized literature.[90]

Legal Requirements for the Use of Force

The most important chapters of the UNC related to the legal requirements for the use of force are chapters six and seven. Chapter six refers to the pacific settlement of disputes whereas chapter seven relates to the actions with respect to threats to peace, breaches of the peace and acts of aggression. Should belligerent parties in a dispute fail to settle it by peaceful means, such as negotiation, enquiry, mediation, conciliation arbitration, judicial settlement or other peaceful means (UNC, Chapter six, Article 33), the SC may investigate any dispute which might lead to international friction. It would do so 'in order to determine whether the circumstance of the dispute or situation is likely to endanger the maintenance of international peace and security.'[91]

If pacific settlement to a dispute is not possible, and the situation likely to imperil international peace and security, the SC can decide measures which shall be taken in accordance with the UNC, Chapter seven, Article 41 and 42. According to Article 41, the SC 'may decide what measures not involving the use of armed forces are to be employed to give effect to its decisions ... These [measures] may include complete or partial interruption of economic relations ... and the severance of diplomatic relations.'[92] Moreover, if Article 41 appears to be inadequate or have proved to be inadequate, the SC may take the decision to use armed forces in order to maintain or restore international peace and security. It is however a myth and nonsense that these military sanctions are the last resort and cannot be taken before Article 41 has been applied by the SC. It depends on the threat presented by a party, especially if this threat is imminent. This aspect will be covered in the chapter dedicated to anticipatory self-defense.

Principles of Necessity and Proportionality

A majority of states agree that a condition for using self defense should be the respect of the principles of necessity and proportionality.[93] However, this condition is not expressed in the UNC, but is established in international customary law - an unwritten body of rules formed from the behavior and opinions of states. Nevertheless, as mentioned in chapter four, preemptive action and the requirements of necessity and proportionality find their origins in the 'Caroline'[94] incident, which occurred in December 1837. The British response was within the limits of international customary law and necessities as well as proportionality were respected. As a report made to the League of Nations in 1927 said: 'Legitimate defense implies the adoption of measures to the seriousness of the attack and justified by the seriousness of the danger.'[95] Proportionality then means to stop and repel an attack.

Until the 'Caroline' case, self defense was a political justification for what, from a legal perspective, were ordinary acts of war. The positivist international law of the 19th century rejected natural law distinctions between just and unjust wars. Military aggression was unregulated and conquest gave good title to territory, as demonstrated by the British acquisition of the Falklands in 1833. The 'Caroline' case did nothing to prevent aggression, but it did draw a legal distinction between war and self-defense. As long as the act being defended against was not itself an act of war, peace would be maintained - a matter of considerable importance to relatively weak countries, as the United States then was.

In the 1981 'Nicaragua' case,[96] the USA stopped economic aid to the left-wing Sandinista Government of Nicaragua because it supported guerrillas fighting against El Salvador's Government, which enjoyed a good relationship with the USA. Nicaragua's Government allowed USSR arms to be passed through its ports and territory en route for El Salvador. The USA, on the ground of collective self defense, used armed force by laying mines in Nicaraguan territorial waters and by attacking ports, naval bases and oil installations. Was the threat against American interests imminent enough to make such preemptive incursions? In the eyes of the Reagan administration, yes, but this view was not shared by those who occupied the International Court of Justice (ICJ).[97]

First of all, Article 51 of the UN Charter stipulates 'armed attack' and in this case, neither an armed attack nor an imminent threat of an armed attack realized by regular armed forces or by irregular armed bands had occurred. Secondly, the ICJ argued that the use of force by the USA was illegal because the actions were not necessary and not proportionate. Thirdly, Article 51 of the UNC also underlines that the exercise of the right of self defense shall be 'immediately reported' to the SC. The absence of a US report was also considered as unlawful. The ICJ provides answers about these problems which can be read in paragraphs 194, 199 and 200 of the judgment.[98]

Article 51 of the UNC specifies that a state can use self defense 'until the Security Council has taken measures necessary to maintain international peace and security.' Some debates have arisen from this unclear temporal element. Does it mean that the self defense stops as soon as the SC seizes the problem or when it makes a decision? To answer this question, it seems appropriate to understand this purpose in the way that the self defense should stop when the SC takes measures, which may be effective or not.

DEDUCTIONS

Article 51 of the UNC authorizes the customary practice of self defense, by using appropriate force although Article 2(4) prohibits the general use of force. Nevertheless, it seems that there is much divergence of practice and interpretation of Article 51 of the UNC, although whatever right of self defense is to be found in the UNC as customary as well as treaty. Some commentators use the US actions such as in Tripoli, Panama, Iraq, and Afghanistan as 'shifting the Charter paradigm and extending the right of self defense.'[99] For example, in the realm of the protection of nationals, few states utilizing the use of force to rescue nationals in a foreign state without the consent of that state, is an illustration of invoking and widening the right of self defense, although it has rarely been practiced. Another example extending the right of self defense is the use of anticipatory self defense, which will be developed in the next section. Nevertheless, the great majority of other states stay rooted in the narrow conception of self defense.

ANTICIPATORY SELF DEFENSE

Legal basis

Some situations occur where, facing an imminent attack, an effective defense implies that the attack has to be anticipated. It is totally reasonable then that the threatened state resorts to the use of armed force and bases its legitimacy on the anticipatory self defense. The spectrum of anticipation has two extremes: at one end there is the natural reflex, 'necessary and determined; at the other end is preventive war, an attack that responds to a distant danger, a matter of foresight and free choice.'[100] Only a few states, such as the USA, Israel and the UK that claim a right under Article 51 of the UNC to protect their nationals also 'claim or defend the right to use force even before their territory or units of their armed forces abroad are attacked.'[101] Formally, the notions of preemption and anticipatory self defense do not appear in the UNC or the ICJ; neither have the SC cautiously provided clear opinion about this particular point. Does it then mean that what is not formally prohibited is permitted? Or does it mean that anticipatory self defense is unlawful?

ARGUMENTATION

Some writers argue for a right of anticipatory self defense, such as Bowett who argues that Article 51 of the UNC 'should safeguard the right of self defense and not restrict it ... No state can be expected to await an initial attack which, in the present state of armaments, may well destroy the state's capacity for further resistance and so jeopardize its very existence.'[102] Other writers argue against this right, such as Kelsen in 1950, Brownlie in 1963 or Henkin in 1979. The latter said that states 'recognized the exception of self defense in emergency, but limited to actual armed attack, which is clear, unambiguous, subject to proof and not open to misinterpretation ... Nations should not be encouraged to strike first under pretext of prevention or preemption.'[103]

The natural focus of writers on controversies where states invoke anticipatory self defense and response to terrorism inevitably gives an unbalanced picture and distorts the perception of state practice. What is exceptional in some cases gives the impression that it is the normal behavior of states like the USA and Israel.

ERICK LABARA

Few states have expressly used anticipatory self defense and its actual invocation in practice is rare. Nevertheless, there are some cases in the history of international law. Israel and South Africa, for example, both have claimed this right by preemptive actions against incursions from neighboring states, but these claims were strongly rejected by some states. Examples have been provided in chapter four to enlighten the reader about this problem such as Israel, when it attacked the Osirak nuclear reactor in Iraq on June 7th 1981; a torrent of virulent condemnations has been discharged against the Israeli state.

Further extensions of anticipatory self defense are the use of force against terrorism. As mentioned in the 'Caroline' case, proportionality means to stop and repel an attack. As far as anticipatory self defense is permitted, proportionality means also to avoid an armed attack. Good illustrations are the actions taken by the USA (for example against Libya in 1986 or against Afghanistan in 2001 [UN Resolution 1373]) and by Israel (for example against Beirut in 1968 or against Tunis in 1985). These actions combine the protection of nationals and anticipatory self defense.

DEDUCTIONS

Israel, relying on the constraints of its geo-political position in the Middle East, frequently referred to anticipatory self defense. This sort of argument is difficult to weigh up. Indeed, it is essential to distinguish between the objective existence of an imminent threat or attack, its true perception and its use as a pretext for starting military operations.

Therefore, preemption against an imminent attack is in fact, a strategy which marries closest to the right of anticipatory self-defense under international law. Although it is not well accepted and subject to many controversies, this strategy is much preferred to prevention, whose threat is not palpable enough to be accepted under Article 51 of the UNC. Indeed, a hostile danger which is not imminent is not a sufficient reason to wage war against an adversary state.

However nowadays, states prefer to invoke self defense rather than to openly claim anticipatory self defense. This is because the latter is firstly not formally mentioned in the UNC, and secondly is rejected by the vast majority of states. Moreover, when a state has invoked anticipatory self defense, it has often been condemned by the SC and the ICJ. Thus, it can be concluded that the right of anticipatory self defense is not formally prohibited, but is indeed not well received, although 'few states claim very wide rights of anticipatory self defense to protect nationals, anticipate attack, and to respond to terrorist and other past attacks.'[104]

WAS THE GULF WAR A JUST WAR?

If this war was preventive, and thus not accepted in international law according to the developments made above, was it nonetheless a so-called 'Just War'? Within a number of obvious contexts the question of legitimacy for engaging in war and the means used have long been preoccupations of scholars, lawyers, theologians, philosophers and politicians alike. 'The basic theory which has arisen within Western culture to evaluate the legitimacy of military action is called "just war theory".'[105]

While it was initially developed early on there came a long period of time in which it remained dormant until, in the Middle

Ages, it recaptured the attention of great thinkers. Emendations to just war theory were first seen in the secular works of the Roman orator and statesman Marcus Tullius Cicero (106 - 43 B.C.), and later, these were elucidated in the religious writings of Hippo of St Augustine (354 - 430) and Thomas Aquinas (1224 - 74). The latter in particular had a profound impact on the elementary core of just war theory.

Afterwards, the Spanish theologians Francisco de Vitoria (1486 - 1546) and Francisco Suarez (1548 - 1617), the Italian jurist Alberico Gentili (1550 - 1608), the Dutch jurist and theologian Hugo Grotius[106] (1583 - 1645), the German political scientist Samuel Pufendorf (1632-1704), the German philosopher and rationalist Christian Wolff (1679-1754) and the Swiss military theorist Emerich de Vattel (1714-1767) all made significant contributions. 'This theory has received widespread acceptance both within Western culture and in the international community as a means by which a war may be determined to be justified or not. Just war theory, which has both religious and secular proponents, is perhaps the most universally recognized moral theory by which the use of force may be evaluated.'[107]

This theory has several commonly recognized elements. Because war was considered a legitimate political tool of sovereign states, there came a major shift in Public Law dealing with the two basic fundamental issues regarding the legitimacy of war.[108] The first issue referred to in Latin as the *jus ad bellum* which literally means 'that which is right or just to engage in resort to war'[109] and is concerned with the appropriateness in resorting to war as a method of conflict resolution. The second issue, *jus in bello*, which literally means 'that which is right or just within war,'[110] deals with what methods of warfare are permissible within the context of a war meeting the criteria of the *jus ad bellum*. When war seems to be inevitable, it should be at least proportionate. Thus, *jus ad bellum* (the just resort to war) and *jus in bello* (the just conduct in war) are traditionally divided in the seven subsequent principles.[111]

The five most common *jus ad bellum* principles are:

> *(1) The cause must be justified.*
>
> *(2) The intention must be right.*
>
> *(3) It must be fought only as the ultimate resort.*
>
> *(4) The war must be waged by a legitimate authority.*
>
> *(5) The war must have a reasonable hope of success.*

The two main *jus in bello* principles are:

> *(6) Discrimination: non-combatants, neutrals and third parties cannot be harmed; moreover existing conventions and treaties, for example the Geneva Convention on the rule of war,[112] must be honored.*
>
> *(7) The means must be proportionate to the goals.*

First, for a war to be just, it must be fought for the right reasons. That is, there must be a just cause with sufficient legal reasoning to back the action taken. 'A decision for war must vindicate justice itself in response to some serious evil, such as an aggressive attack.'[113] An example of this is the action taken against Afghanistan by the USA and its allies to address the 'seriousness' which was the Taliban and its harboring of terrorist sub-state organizations. In international law this concept is mirrored in Article 51 of the UNC. However, therein lays a problem: the notion of imminence as argued above is simply not addressed.

Second, in fighting a war, the goal must be to do that which is necessary to obtain peace. Therefore, the war must be fought with the right intention. This means that the motives for the war must not be to inflict excessive suffering on the enemy state. The principle of right intention is narrowly linked with the first principle of just causes. 'The defending nation must use only that amount of force which is necessary for it to achieve its just cause.'[114] The motives of those engaged in making the decision to go to war 'must not be tinged with vengeance or a desire for retribution.'[115]

Third, and besides right intention, war must be the last resort, or better said, the ultimate resort. As soon as diplomacy and economic measures have been used as other resorts and are exhausted, then the use of force as the ultimate resort is possible.

Forth, it must be waged under rightful and competent authority, that is, states, and states only, not groups or influential individuals, because the former are sovereign. It is necessary for a war to be waged under lawful authority; Warfare which is declared by unlawful authority therefore fails to meet the criteria, as does warfare which is not directed towards peace and the common good.

Fifth, there must be a reasonable hope of success: the end (result) must be better than the means. For example, one cannot definitely destroy something he has to protect.

Sixth, *jus in bello* requires that there must be limited objectives and discrimination between civilian and military targets which are usually defined by the competent authority and endorsed by the international community, preferably the UN. Finally, 'the amount of damage inflicted must be strictly proportionate to the ends sought. Injuries should not be avenged by massive suffering, death, and devastation. The war's harm must not exceed the war's good.'[116] In order to answer the question 'Was Gulf War III a Just War?' these seven elements have to be examined.

1) *IUSTA CAUSA* (JUST CAUSE)

According to Thomas Aquinas quoting Hippo of St Augustine, 'a just war is wont to be described as one that avenges wrongs, when a nation or state has to be punished, for refusing to make amends for the wrongs inflicted by its subjects, or to restore what it has seized unjustly.'[117] The first principle of *iusta causa* is however subject to controversy because possessing just cause is the first and arguably the most important condition. Today, some would argue that 'given that there have been no "smoking guns" found in Iraq, there is good reason to doubt after the fact that the American-British attack was a just war. On the other hand, given the brutal nature of the Saddam Hussein regime, it is difficult to argue that the Iraqi people would have been better off under his continued rule.'[118] Even so, it is always easy to bring up such arguments because smoking guns are very likely to exist but have not been found yet. One of the main reasons is simple: Iraq is a large nation and had had several years to hide its WMD arsenal. Consider how difficult it was to find Saddam Hussein – a single man – who remained on the lamb for nearly six months. When the despot was finally captured, it was found that he had been hiding in a small hole strategically built into the ground and very well hidden. Imagine the volume of chemicals or biological material that could have been dissimulated in a similar space that had been camouflaged in a similar manner; locating WMD in Iraq is tantamount to finding a needle in a hay stack. The fact that it has not been found does not negate the potential danger or threat that they pose to the security of the USA and its allies. Therefore, it is tremendously naïve to believe that in the relatively short period of time between the years 1998 and 2002 – where there were no UN weapons inspectors in the country to hold Saddam Hussein accountable to binding UN resolutions – the dictator would, without providing proof, spontaneously volunteer to destroy his arsenal.

In addition to his failure to comply with the UN, intelligence reports provided ample evidence of mobile and static WMD sites for producing these weapons. And while not posing a *per se* imminent threat, his failures coupled with these reports gave credence to the US led invasion as a *just cause* war. Furthermore, these reports indicated that Saddam Hussein was pursuing the development of nuclear weapons that could potentially be used against America and its allies. The real problem then, according to Dr. Condoleezza Rice, was that there would always be some measure of uncertainty about how quickly Saddam could acquire nuclear weapons. In fact, prior to the war she made the statement '[W]e don't want the smoking gun to be a mushroom cloud,' [119] which is apropos to this argument. Thus, the USA not only had good reason to wage war because of the foregoing facts - which obviously meet the first principle of just war theory – but they were also given cause to do so in an effort to prevent future ties between the Iraqi regime and terrorist sub-state organizations so as to thwart additional mass slaughters confirmed by the existence of mass graves discovered during 2003.

2) *RECTA INTENTIO* (RIGHT INTENTION)

Intent is right when its objectives are to promote or secure peace by overthrowing a threat towards peace, protecting life of innocent people, restoring political independency and sovereignty of a state and eventually assuring the very existence of the state and its people. Thus, the destruction of WMD and their facilities which are in the hands of a despot is legitimate, especially if the individual had no scruples in using them against another country or against his own population, which in fact is exactly what Saddam Hussein did in the first Gulf War against Iran and later against the Kurds in April 1988, respectively. In consequence, the second principle defined as 'right intention' is met: the right intention was to topple Saddam Hussein and his sons and to destroy the facilities manufacturing WMD.

3) *ULTIMA RATIO* (ULTIMATE RESORT)

Requirements are also met for the third principle named as last or ultimate resort. Diplomatic efforts, preventive diplomacy and economic measures, weapon inspections as well as former UN resolutions have not been successful enough to ease the situation. War was the ultimate resort, although some states,[120] especially France and Germany, viewed by the USA with an amused tolerance, have argued that other preventive means could have been used.

4) *LEGITIMA AUCTORITAS* (LEGITIMATE AUTHORITIES)

As competent authorities are states, the forth principle is obviously met. Nevertheless, one can argue that the UN represents a body of states and thus should have been the rightful and competent authority to allow the use of force against Iraq, which was not the case. Therefore, it can be deduced that, according to international law, the forth principle has not been met, but, as said before, the right of (anticipatory) self-defense acknowledges that exercising this right does not mean absorbing a devastating first blow. Indeed, 'if waiting for imminence means waiting until it is no longer possible to act effectively, the victim is left no alternative to suffering the first blow.'[121]

5) REASONABLE HOPE OF SUCCESS

'A decision for war must be based on a prudent expectation that the ends sought can be achieved. It is hardly an act of justice to plunge one's people into the suffering and sacrifice of a suicidal conflict.'[122] The overwhelming power of the US-led armed forces have led to a reasonable hope of success, destroying what they wanted to, and trying with success to protect what they needed to. This satisfies the fifth principle.

6) AND 7) *JUS IN BELLO* (DISCRIMINATION AND PROPORTIONALITY)

The overthrowing of Saddam's regime and the destruction of Iraqi facilities manufacturing WMD of limited objectives meet consequently the sixth and seventh principles because the US attempted to discriminate, quite successfully and with a certain degree of proportionality, combatant from non-combatant targets. Indeed, the humanitarian catastrophe predicted by various international bodies did not occur as expected:

mass migrations did not take place and biological and chemical weapons have not been used. Moreover, the level of urban combat predicted did not come to fruition, which could have had dramatic humanitarian consequences.

DEDUCTIONS

It is this author's opinion that if one were to objectively examine the events that proceeded and directly followed the Third Gulf War, including examining the intelligence presented at the time as being accurate, against the criteria of recognized *Just War Theory*, all of the tests have been met. This included the first test, which is the most controversial. At the beginning of the war there was sufficient evidence to support international concerns that Iraq was producing WMD against binding UN resolutions. Further, there was both a moral and legal imperative for the international community to investigate and take action to prevent Saddam Hussein from committing further human rights violations. This coupled with the allegation that he may have had links to terrorist sub-state organizations, supported preemptive action. Thus, it is appropriate to examine these prevailing factors in the following chapter.

ALTERNATIVE MAIN COURSE

Wok Végétarien

For those of you who love and 'prefer vegetables, this special dish comprises tasty mushrooms, onions, and other fresh garden ingredients and Provencal herbs combined in a wok with a splash of something special.

Please now turn briefly to the fifth photograph located in the center of the book. Remember also that these recipes and more can be found at ***www.wonderfood.biz*** and of course my own website ***www.ericklabara.com***.

"A just war is apt to be described as one that avenges wrongs, when a nation or state has to be punished, for refusing to make amends for the wrongs inflicted by its subjects, or to restore what has been seized unjustly."

Saint Augustine in Aquinas' Summa Theoligica

CHAPTER SIX
PREEMPTION:
A NEW STRATEGY
IN THE SECURITY
PARADIGM?

La raison du plus fort est toujours la meilleure.' [123]
(Translation: the reason of the strongest is always the best one.)

Jean de la Fontaine (1621-95)

'The object of war is not to die for your country but to make the other bastard die for his.' [124]

General George Patton (1885-1945)

The Spectrum of Prevention and Conflict

As demonstrated in chapter five, preemptive war is then justified by an imminent and real threat of attack, a clear present danger that a threatening country is about to attack another country and thus to endanger international security. In such a case a preemptive attack is recognized as justifiable under international law. Nevertheless, international norms require that non-military options should be exhausted before considering military instruments. As underlined in Article 33 of the UNC, the parties to any dispute 'shall first of all, seek a solution by negotiation, enquiry, mediation, conciliation, arbitration, judicial settlement, resort to regional agencies or arrangements, or other peaceful means of their own choice.'[125] Therefore, the use of force should be the instrument of ultimate resort. The panoply of non-military preventive instruments that can be used to avoid imminent threat and violent conflict is various.

First, early warning and response (for example through the conjunction of governments, non-governmental agencies, international organizations and traditional diplomacy) correlated with strong leadership and support, by the UNSC for example, can be enough to provide the necessary solutions to a security problem. Thus, preventive efforts and responses can 'create the basic conditions to encourage moderation and make responsible political control possible.'[126] Nevertheless, during the early stages of a crisis, policymakers should not only pay attention to how circumstances could worsen, but also be looking for opportunities to make constructive use of local issues and processes.

Second is preventive diplomacy, by using ambassadors, senior foreign office officials and UN personnel. When a situation worsens, states usually 'suspend diplomatic relations as a
substitute for action.'[127] Diplomatic relations should therefore
remain open in order to create constructive solutions for re-
solving a crisis. Quiet diplomacy as well as open and honest
dialogue should maintain the trust of all parties. Furthermore,
it is essential to help mobilize support for preventive action
and to use forceful measures in order to be clear against unac-
ceptable behavior. As Sun Tzu said by emphasizing the excel-
lence of diplomacy and intelligence in trying to avoid conflicts:
'To win one hundred victories in one hundred battles is not
the acme of skill. To subdue the enemy without fighting is the
acme of skill.'[128]

Third, economic measures, such as sanctions or incentives
play an important role in supporting preventive diplomacy.
The use of sanctions serves 'to signal international concern to
the offending state, to punish a state's behavior and to serve
as an important precursor to stronger actions, including, if
necessary, the use of force.'[129] These conditional measures are
a signal to the 'belligerent' state that tougher action could be
forthcoming if corrective steps are not taken.

Fourth, the threat or use of force will arise in situations where
dialogues, diplomatic prevention or even economic measures
are insufficient to prevent the outbreak or recurrence of a major conflict. The question is 'when, where and how should nations, global and regional organizations be willing to apply
forceful measures to curb incipient violence and prevent potentially much larger destruction of life and property.'[130] Three

basic principles should govern any such decision: any threat or use of force must be governed by universally accepted principles (as the UNC requires), should not be regarded only as the last resort in frantic circumstances but as the ultimate resort.[131] Moreover, it 'must be part of an integrated, ideally multilateral strategy, and used in conjunction with political and economic instruments.'[132] In addition, when employing force for preventive or preemptive purposes, states should only do so with a UNSC resolution specifying a clear mandate that details the arrangements under which force should be used. Nevertheless, in practice, multilateral decisions endorsed by the UNSC authorizing the use of force have been rare. In contemporary history, only the Second Gulf War (1991) with its relating resolutions,[133] and the war against the Taliban regime in Afghanistan had clear UN backing (UN Resolution 1373 of September 28th 2001).[134]

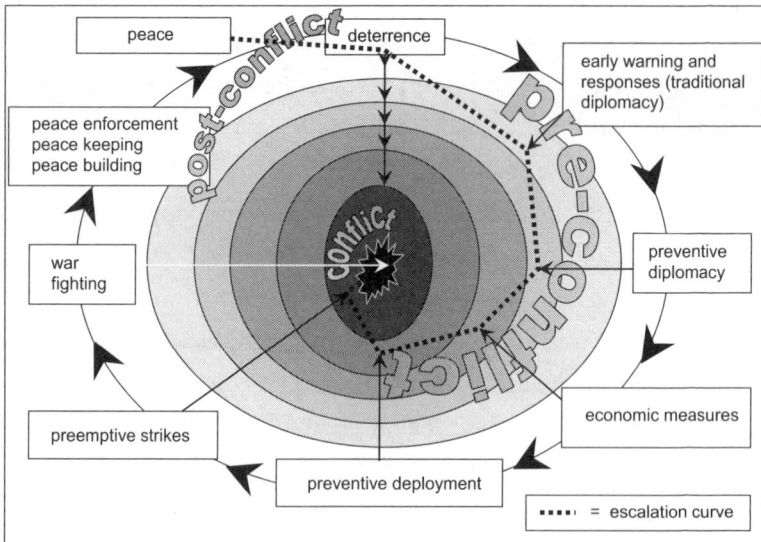

Diagram 1: The Spectrum of Preventive Measures and Conflicts
Source: Author

Diagram 1 allows the reader to gain a global picture of the considerations developed above.

DEDUCTIONS

It can be deduced that preemption appears to be another face of the changing security paradigm, but it is one of many means dealing with security like deterrence, preventive diplomacy, economical measures such as sanctions and incentives. However, the record of international crises reveals the need in certain cases to respond rapidly and with force. This option should be considered within three basic principles: first, any threat or use of force must be governed by universally accepted principles, as the UN Charter requires. Second the threat or use of force should be regarded as the ultimate resort and third, this option must be part of an integrated, ideally multilateral strategy, and used in conjunction with political and economic instruments.

In the case of Iraq (2003), several UN resolutions, especially UN Resolution 1441 have been disregarded by Saddam Hussein's regime, and just for this reason, a war was justified. Moreover, the threat posed by the manufacturing of WMD represented a hostile danger, though not imminent, to international peace and security. In addition, the withdrawal of weapons inspectors in 1998 from Iraq might suggest that the Iraqi regime had continued to produce CBRN weapons. Indeed, it is very hard to imagine - as both President George W. Bush and Prime Minister Tony Blair argued forcefully - 'that the regime of Iraqi President Saddam Hussein would have abandoned that effort in the four years after the inspectors withdrew.'[135] The unsuccessful outcome of diplomatic pressure and economic sanctions as well as UN influence led to war. 'But the principle of using force only after exhausting non-military alternatives necessarily implies a willingness to recognize that, at some point, they have been exhausted, and that waiting too long may mean waiting until military options are no longer effective at acceptable costs.'[136] The decision to wage a war, especially a preventive one, should ideally be made on a multilateral basis and must be made by international institutions, preferably the UN. Unfortunately, this was not the case because the international community assessed the Iraqi WMD threat as too vague and not imminent at all, despite US and British intelligence reports, the latter being covered later in this chapter. In fact, preventive war, is not only a violation of international law, but an 'unbounded invitation to use of force on mere suspicion of the ambitions or intent of another nation; it is indeed a negation of the very concept of international law.'[137]

INITIATIVE, UNILATERALISM AND STRATEGIC SURPRISE

There were two great surprises associated with the events of September 11th 2001. One was the event itself, which certainly surprised everybody. These events arrived in an unexpected way at an unexpected time against an unexpected target and the USA was not prepared at all for such an extraordinary and audacious attack. The second great surprise that emerged from September 11th was the quick and successful counterattack of the USA against the Taliban regime in Afghanistan.

As Hans Bachofner once wrote, 'people who now continue to plan on the basis of security policies and strategies of the 1990s have not understood the signals of September 11th 2001. What was called 'modern' yesterday is today out of date. The war against the Taliban regime in Afghanistan was neither an episode nor the finality. This war was the beginning of a long lasting, world-wide mission involving several states' vehicles for combating newly emerging threats.'[138] Thus, it was for certain that the twelve-year holiday of history (1990 - 2001) had come to an end.

'Since the events of September 2001, humanity has entered a sustained case of seriousness. These events have swept the ideological imagination of military planning people who were searching for peace dividends by unfortunately reducing military forces budgets, civil protection and defense.'[139] Security needed a rethink and to be implemented in new strategies, which advocated the old principles of initiative and surprise. Therefore, an adjustment of the US NSS was a necessary step to respond to new threats, especially asymmetric ones. Indeed, the terrible consequences of the mass-casualty attacks of September 11th 2001 on the USA have elevated military preemption as a US policy option. Nevertheless, US Secretary of State Colin Powell had stressed the continuity of this policy by saying that 'preemption remains part of a spectrum of means, including non-military instruments, which the USA will continue to employ.'[140] The reality is that national super-powers and the collective efforts of the United Nations have, to some degree, been given the role of "world policemen" by default. The expectation of the international community is that the USA and other wealthy countries use that wealth and their power to effect positive change and to help democracy take hold worldwide. This gives some additional credence to a strategy of preemption. Of course, critics of this doctrine have not failed to castigate the mutation of the US's strategic mission, especially regarding the war against Saddam Hussein in 2003. The usual reproaches concerning US unilateralism and imperialism has added to the fear that the whole structure of international relations would collapse, provoked a genuine fear of international instability. New doubts about the notions of national sovereignty and self-defense have been raised. But does this mean that the longsuffering assembly of international relations crowned in 1945 by the UNC is suddenly threatened? It is true that 'the presentation of the preemption policy has generated controversy and apprehension, particularly among America's European allies'[141] and has provoked turmoil in the international community. Nevertheless, the credibility of the UN was at stake when, in one of the most powerful speeches of his presidency, President George W. Bush warned the General Assembly of the UN on September 12th 2002 'that Saddam's twelve-year defiance of the Security Council resolutions threatened the credibility and fundamental viability of the UN system.'[142] The eight weeks of negotiations that followed this speech culminated, on November 8th 2002, in the SC's unanimous adoption of UN Resolution 1441.

It can therefore be deduced that the seizing of initiative at strategic level was fruitful for the US because the UNSC adopted UN Resolution 1441 unanimously. Moreover, according to the US and UK assessment of threat posed by the Iraqi regime of Saddam Hussein, implementing the new US NSS was indirectly sustained and accepted by the UN. The strategic outcome for the USA has been remarkable.

'We must prevent the terrorists and regimes who seek chemical, biological, or nuclear weapons from threatening the United States and the world ... I will not wait on events, while dangers gather.'[143] This sentence in the speech of President Bush on January 29th 2002 also places the importance of the US seizing the initiative at a strategic level. In addition, it confirmed indirectly the continuation of US NSS policy under the Clinton administration which described the decision of employing military force as following: 'We act in concert with the international community, whenever possible, but do not hesitate to act unilaterally if necessary.'[144] As mentioned above, the decision on use of military forces should ideally be made on a multilateral basis, but 'there is, however, in international law - and more in international practice - widespread acceptance of the concept that, in the end, all decisions on use of military forces are unilateral.'[145] However, such decisions must be made in light of the opinions and interest of the international community in order to gain its support.

According to international practice, numerous nations, themselves adherent of a multilateral approach, have proven, nevertheless, 'ready to use their military forces for their national aims without bothering much about international opinion, as Spain did last summer over the occupation of a disputed Mediterranean island.'[146] Moreover, Germany to take another example, though adept at multilateral decisions about the use of force, insists 'on reserving the right to make a separate national decision on whether a multilateral approval of military action is sufficiently justified -or sufficiently serves its own nation's goals and principles - to require actually participating in the action.'[147]

Yet initiative and strategic surprise are, as usual, the basis of every strategy and war preparations, and are narrowly linked together. The events of September 11th have also called into question the concept of collective security. 'Who on September 11th had more partners and allies, tremendous influence on international organizations, lots of intelligence agencies on duty, and more armed forces dispersed throughout the globe than the USA? Who was assuredly at best protected from 'rogue states' and terrorists than the USA?'[148] The nice and well-sounding left-wing speeches such as 'we are all friends and we believe in universal peace and freedom' sound dreadful in the wake of the September 11th attacks. 'International organizations, thus, cannot guarantee peace. The reverse is true: it is because peace reigned, that international organizations have flourished.'[149] Therefore the need of initiative and strategic surprise, preferably with UN backing, and sometimes unilateralism represent the guarantor for future international peace and security. As Clausewitz said, 'Surprise therefore becomes the means to gain superiority.'[150] In order to gain superiority, intelligence is needed and this vital aspect will be covered in the next chapter.

THE VITAL ROLE OF INTELLIGENCE

President Bush said in his impressive speech on June the 1st 2002, 'Our security will require the best intelligence, to reveal threats hidden in caves and growing in laboratories. Our security will require modernizing domestic agencies such as the FBI, so they're prepared to act, and act quickly, against danger.'[151] The first operational issue about preemptive is whether the proposed operation will actually eliminate the threat targeted. Therefore, intelligence is paramount before any political or military operation can be launched. In order to understand the task of intelligence, it is important now to define it. Intelligence is 'processed, accurate information, presented in sufficient time to enable a decision-maker to take whatever action is required.'[152]

As mentioned at the end of chapter three, the permanent challenge for intelligence communities is to assess threats. Threat (T) is the factor of the enemy's capabilities (C) and its intentions (I): ($T = C \times I$). An enemy's capabilities are quite easy to assess, because they can be quantified, as it was in the Iraqi case. If the capabilities of the Iraqi state were accurately assessed is another question. However, the enemy's intentions are much more difficult to assess, as this represents a qualitative factor subject to the subjectivity of the assessor. Indeed, it is very difficult to evaluate the ideas and plans of an enemy, unless clear and undoubted evidence is demonstrated, but it is still not always obvious to perceive its exact intent. Thus the assessment of threats requires very accurate intelligence.

Intelligence, then, is information that has been systematically and professionally processed and analyzed. In order to better understand the intelligence process, it is now worth enlighten-

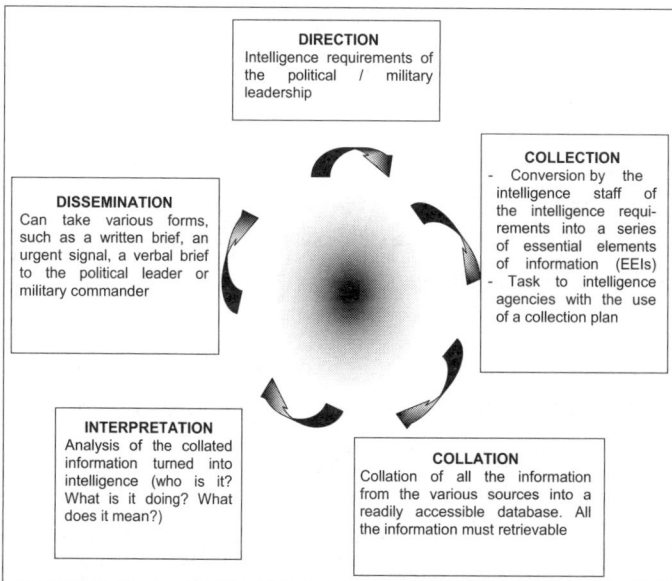

Diagram 2: The Intelligence Cycle
Source: John Hughes-Wilson, Military Intelligence Blunders, (Constable Publishers, London, 1999), p.6

ing the reader about the functioning of intelligence with the help of the diagram 2, which represents the intelligence cycle.

SOURCES AND TYPES OF INTELLIGENCE

Intelligence communities have at their disposal several different methods of gathering information vital to national security. Usually, these methods fall into the two broad categories called technical intelligence (TECHINT) and human intelligence (HUMINT). These are also known as sources. TECHINT is subdivided in the three main categories: imagery intelligence (IMINT), signals intelligence (SIGINT) and electronic intelligence (ELINT). Another source of intelligence, included in TECHINT and HUMINT is known as open source (or non-classified) intelligence (OSINT). It is however worth stressing that by some estimates, 'sixty percent of intelligence comes from unclassified sources' (OSINT and HUMINT).[153] These methods of intelligence collection are utilized synergistically when seeking to protect their country from terrorism and monitoring the world for proliferation of WMD. The questions that need to be answered in gathering intelligence are called 'essential elements of information' and can be found in a matrix which illustrates a collection plan. The subsequent simplistic and non-exhaustive example, shows how a collection plan works. See table 3.

Other sources can provide valuable information as well. An example of this is the *Schlesinger Working Group on Strategic Surprises* which intends 'to review and assess a range of possible scenarios that contain significant potential for strategic surprise and unanticipated outcomes. The initiative aims to identify future crisis areas, as well as unexpected events and political and economic discontinuities around the globe.'[154]

ERICK LABARA

Sources and Agencies	HUMINT	SIGINT	IMAGERY	DIPLOMATIC	MILITARY	ALLIES	OSINT
EEIs	e.g. CIA (US) MI6 (UK) SVR*	e.g. NSA (US) GCHQ (UK) FAPSI*	e.g. NRO (US) JARIC (UK)	e.g. Foreign & Commonwealth Office, attachés State Department	e.g. DIA (US) DIS (UK) GRU*	e.g. US / UK NATO	e.g. CNN Internet
Where are the facilities manufacturing WMD?	✓		✓	✓	✓		
Where are WMD being deposit?			✓	✓			
How many WMD are in the country?	✓			✓	✓	✓	✓
Is there any evidence of WMD being displaced?	✓		✓	✓			✓
What is their government's official line?		✓		✓		✓	✓
Evidence of civilian mobilisation?	✓	✓	✓	✓			✓
...							

* Russia

Table 3: Intelligence Collection Plan's Essential Elements of Information (EEI)
Source: Author

Once the information has been collected, it is then collated. In other words, the information is put together so it can be analyzed. 'This can be laborious and unglamorous, but the greater part of the intelligence operative's work'[155] is in the collation process. Nowadays, the collation system and all records are computerized, which makes the process infinitely more efficient.

Once collated, the information has to be interpreted and evaluated. In this process, all information is compared with any other existing information in order to answer four basic questions: Is it true? Who is it? What is it doing? What does it mean? In other words, the information must be verified; is it relevant, reliable, credible, and accurate. Afterwards, the information is meticulously evaluated.

The final part of the intelligence cycle is the dissemination of relevant, reliable, credible and accurate information to selected recipients. 'Dissemination, then should be accurate, timely and clearly distinguish intelligence fact from interpretative comment or assessment. It should also be secure and free from prying eyes.'[156]

As mentioned above, the primary task of intelligence is to throw light on the political or military decision. However, there are different types of intelligence.[157] First, investigative intelligence aims to gather information which explains an event. This is currently called police intelligence, which collects clues on events, objects, organizations and people. This type of intelligence demands significant collection efforts as well as great care. Second, documentation intelligence aims to create a record of references, which is used to support routine decisions. This intelligence should be sufficiently rich to reduce the need of EEI in the event of a crisis and is a normal activity in all intelligence communities, which can take various shapes according to the nature of the community.

Finally, anticipatory intelligence is related to future events and this is the most complex, demanding and hazardous type of intelligence. Indeed, it should enable decisions to be taken about non tangible though foreseeable incidents, and demands high analytical and abstract abilities. Furthermore, qualified personnel for this kind of intelligence are not easy to find which makes intelligence communities hesitant to get involved in anticipatory intelligence. Indeed, future threats are not tangible enough to assess them with accuracy and political maneuvering is often required when such intelligence is sought from the public and the media. Anticipatory intelligence is a task at the strategic level and bases itself on the two other types of intelligence. Again, they are all synergistic parts of the whole; they work in concert. 'The understanding of these three types of intelligence is paramount to define the services' orientation, their capabilities and the profile of their agents.'[158] In addition, it should help manage and integrate interactions between the various services in the global realm of intelligence. The latter has to organize its services in such a way that they avoid duplication of effort, the squandering of their resources, and/or the engagement if superfluous activities.

SPECTRUM OF THREATS

WMD

In order to preempt or prevent future threats, it is essential to convince the international community of their likelihood. Intelligence must therefore be reliable, believable and provable as its sources and agencies. With regard to the 2003 Iraqi case, the USA and the UK had assessed the Iraqi threat by alluding to the danger of WMD and their manufacture, and the alleged support by Saddam Hussein's regime of terrorist organizations such as Al Qaeda. Indeed, the British intelligence report *Iraq's Weapons of Mass Destruction, The Assessment of the British Government* (See Appendix B), indicated that as part of Iraq's military planning Saddam Hussein's regime was willing to use chemical and biological weapons, including against it own Shia population, as was the case in April 1988 when Saddam Hussein's regime attacked its own Kurdish population.[159] Moreover, the report stipulated that the Iraqi military were 'able to deploy chemical or biological weapons within 45 minutes of an order to do so.'[160] It is precisely these 45 minutes, in the assessment of US and British intelligence, which justified a preemptive war. Nevertheless, as developed in chapter four, this threat albeit very real, was not imminent although intelligence also had confirmed that Saddam Hussein had continued to make progress with its illicit weapons programs and judged that Iraq was continuing to produce chemical and biological agents. Moreover, US Secretary of State Colin Powell's presentation to the UN General Assembly on February 5th 2003 regarding Iraq's alleged WMD program simply did not carry sufficient weight to convince the international community.

During the late spring 2003, the British intelligence report was the prey of scathing attacks by critics, who asserted that this dossier was not accurate enough to justify the war against Iraq. Indeed, it was said that this report was an amalgam between Internet sources and other information gathered by intelligence services. MI6 was heavily criticized about its own credibility and reliability. The British Government immediately admitted it should have been more careful when it drew up a dossier of intelligence information before the war in Iraq.[161] Tony Blair's adviser Alastair Campbell promised MI6 that far greater care would be taken with its work in future. He has ordered a tightening of procedures after the criticism heaped on the so-called 'dodgy dossier'. Therefore, this dossier should never have been published because what was an honest appraisal seems to have turned into a thorn in the side of the British Government.

Nevertheless, waiting for an Iraqi WMD attack or allowing Saddam Hussein to get even closer to possessing a nuclear weapon were not acceptable options. The option proposed by France, Germany and Russia at the start of 2003 to enable further inspections could have been possible, but considering Saddam Hussein's past record of deception, inspections would have taken months, if not years, to verify the existence and extent of these programs. Moreover, Iraq was suspected of having mobile laboratories[162] that are constantly changing locations and deeply buried bunkers housing WMD. Given this constraint, UN inspectors may never have been able to prove the existence of Iraqi WMD programs and arsenals.

During the 1991-1998 inspections, many of the important discoveries occurred because of information shared by Iraqi defectors. Although UN Resolution 1441 allowed relevant Iraqi scientists and their families to be interviewed outside of the country, realistically, such interviews are not easy to organize or to implement.

Inside or outside of Iraq, Iraqi scientists who would have agreed to be interviewed would have endangered not only their own lives, but also those of their immediate and extended family members. Thus, inspectors may have found that this option was not workable.

Alleged Links of Saddam Hussein with Al Qaeda

It was asserted before the war and following it to this day that the Iraqi regime had links with the terrorist organization Al Qaeda, but there were no hard facts to prove it. Make no mistake about it intelligence agencies had a very difficult task here. Indeed, 'intelligence information is the first line of defense against political terrorism. The organizational structures, methods of operation, and political objectives of terrorist groups must be fully understood by police and government authorities.'[163] This task is quite difficult since terrorist organizations try to keep actions secret in order to ensure the advantage of the element of surprise. Such organizations, without the borders and assets that define nations, do not always operate in a way that enables high-technology collection methods.

Most TECHINT methods of intelligence are designed to target a state's infrastructure and this makes these assets only marginally successful against the threat of terrorists. SIGINT and IMINT collection are good examples of this.

The National Security Agency (NSA) has achieved some success in intercepting conversations made by Al Qaeda's leader Osama Bin Laden in the past but more recent efforts to monitor Al Qaeda's terrorist network have not been productive with SIGINT means[164] because the terrorist organization has considerably improved their discipline in communications. IMINT has had similar results. The aerial imagery of the Zhawar Kili Al-Badr terrorist training camp in Afghanistan facilitated a U.S. cruise missile attack in 1998.[165] Nevertheless, IMINT can be defeated by disappearing from its visual spectrum, for example by moving underground or changing location very frequently. This reveals the importance of HUMINT. An example of this may be when double-agents infiltrate a regime. This is the most valuable intelligence role and is more effective than any other method of intelligence gathering in fighting terrorism. The reality is that only 'authorized' people will have known if Saddam had links with Al Qaeda and if this is not the case, the answer could only be given by Saddam and Bin Laden themselves.

Human Rights Abuses

'Our quarrel is with Saddam, not the Iraqi people. They deserve better. Iraq is a country with a very talented population, a country that is potentially rich and successful. We want to welcome it back into the international community. We want the people to be free to live fulfilling lives without the oppression and terror of Saddam.'[166] As Prime Minister Tony Blair stressed, the Iraqi people were in constant fear of being tortured by being denounced as opponents of Saddam's regime. Torture was systematic in Iraq and most senior figures were personally involved. Arbitrary arrests and killings were commonplace. According to *Amnesty International's 10-point appeal* of April 22, 2003, 'there is an urgent need to protect human rights in Iraq.'[167] Although major combat operations officially ended on May 1st 2003, violence, killings, destruction of property and widespread insecurity has continued, and the humanitarian emergency still remains (July 2003). 'If Iraq's future is to be hopeful, it must be built on respect for human rights.'[168]

Although the US and the UK have not specified human rights abuses as the major threat, it was also a factor to the decision to wage a war against Iraq. Unfortunately, the argument of human right abuses was not put forward as one of the major threats to international peace and security, as the international community had closed its eyes for more than two decades. Nevertheless, such a threat, besides the one posed by WMD and alleged links to terrorist organizations, was indeed provable, credible, reliable and believable, and could have convinced more people and media about the soundness of this war.

DEDUCTIONS

Shortly after September 11th 2001, US intelligence services were harshly criticized for their failure to predict the event. Indeed, detractors have denounced that 'technical collection systems have been used to the detriment of human intelligence.'[169] This assertion is far from accurate. At the end of the Cold War, the USA placed their intelligence focus on fighting organized crime and drug-trafficking which was having a terribly negative impact on the nation and indeed the world. The infiltration of such complex networks has required an increased recruitment of personnel from specific ethnic groups so that infiltration would be possible, but this does not happen overnight. It is a long and arduous process requiring not only months but quite possibly years to accomplish. '[T]he setting up of HUMINT is a long and exacting task, moreover complex due to the multiplicity of threats and variety of networks.'[170] On the other hand, the infiltration of simple networks operating with close confidants where the notion of hierarchy is strong is very difficult if not totally impossible to infiltrate.

Prediction such events are also tremendously if not completely impossible to predict. Although international intelligence exchange may tend to assess threats more reliably, and gathering all possible information and sources, as accurate they might be, it is very rare that intelligence services can predict an event with absolute certainty. Intelligence is a process using intellect and analysis, it is not clairvoyance. The process resides and functions in the real world not in the supernatural. Thus, it is subject to natural laws and confined to the abilities of normal human beings.

ABOUT PREEMPTION AND PREVENTION

The significance of the 2002 US NSS document is contained in chapter 5, entitled 'Prevent Our Enemies from Threatening Us, Our Allies, and Our Friends with Weapons of Mass Destruction,'[171] which underlines the concept of preventive and preemptive action. The first issue with these doctrines is to assess accurately the intentions of a potential enemy willing to use WMD. The second is whether the submitted operation will indeed eliminate the WMD capability targeted. To know what and where to strike and to know enough about a nation's WMD programs to have sufficient confidence of destroying them by preemptive is the problem that intelligence has to resolve. 'Precision weapons require precision intelligence, and preemptive requires that intelligence be comprehensive as well as precise.'[172] Still more difficult is dealing with the potential response of an enemy, even if his WMD capability has been successful eliminated.

In the North Korean case, deterrence apparently works. Nevertheless, the North Korean missile and nuclear programs are much more advanced that those of Iraq. Moreover, it has an active program of selling its weapons technology to others. 'There is no question about the location of the plutonium-production reactor and re-processing facility at Yongbyon, and as former Secretary of Defence William Perry has written, the US military has the capability to destroy them quickly and without release of radioactive materials.'[173] Nevertheless, if the North Korean capability of Yongbyon is not stopped in the near future, it might be too late, and the world as well as the region will have to deal with a regime armed with powerful WMD capability that can neither be pre-empted nor defended against. In addition, North Korea has 'massive conventional forces - and there is no chance that this capability could be eliminated preemptively, even by a massive effort.'[174]

ASSESSING THE THREATS

The assessment of threats and possible evolutions is the permanent task of intelligence. Especially after September 11th, the interpretation of Cold War threats is overtaken, however not obsolete. This interpretation is reflected in the 2002 US NSS in chapter 5,[175] and deals with symmetrical threats and conflicts. Now, instead of this, it is asymmetrical ones that haunt policy makers. 'With great powers less inclined to threaten each other, threats are likely to come from far weaker powers, which might be inclined to use unconventional means to compensate for their inferior conventional military capabilities.'[176] The range of such possible evolutions involving so-called rogue states and sub-state terrorist organizations which threaten peace and security is represented in diagram 3.

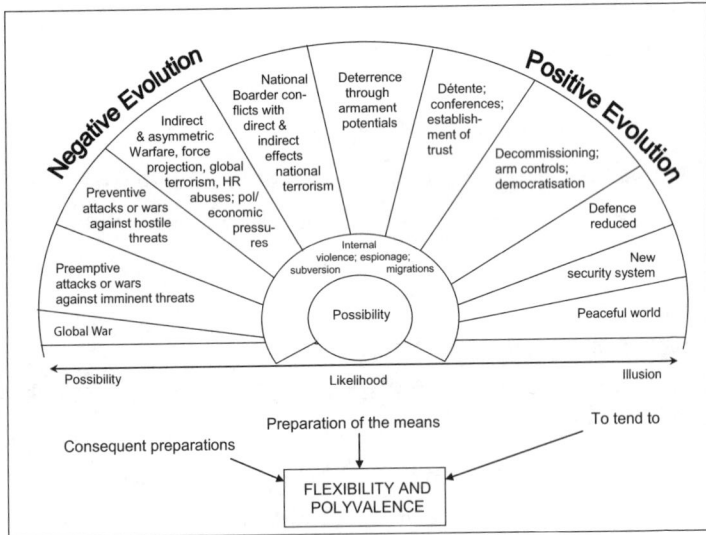

Diagram 3: *The Fan of Possible Evolutions*
Source: Author

AFTER DINNER

Plateau de fromages

No meal would be complete without a serving of hard, soft, and fresh cheeses made from cow's, goat's or even ewe's milk served with herbs and spices to tantalize your taste buds.

Please now turn briefly to the sixth photograph located in the center of the book. Remember also that these recipes and more can be found at **www.wonderfood.biz** and of course my own website **www.ericklabara.com**.

"Being against the war was yesterday's argument: today the only question is whether you are for or against victory."

Herald Sun columnist Andrew Bolt

CHAPTER SEVEN
CONCLUSION

'War is never an isolated act.' [177]

Carl von Clausewitz (1780 - 1831)

SUMMARY

The title of this book is: 'Preemptive War' and there is probably no straightforward answer to the question of whether preemptive is justifiable or not. It always depends on the context. Nevertheless, this study has tried to illustrate the problem by providing answers and personal deductions within the objectives described in chapter one.

Chapter one has introduced the subject by presenting the various controversies which have been further developed throughout this book. It has been shown that preemption has taken an important place in the new US NSS in order to fight new emerging threats. It has also described the aim and objectives which have been covered in the six subsequent chapters.

Chapter two has given a succinct overview of available historical, legal and philosophical literature relating to books, journals, reports, official documents and the Internet. Without citing all literature read, it has identified the gaps which have then been hopefully filled in this book.

Chapter three has explored in depth the definitions related to the words of preemption and prevention. It has also given a theoretical example in order to enlighten the reader about the subtlety of these two notions. Preemption is related to the action taken because of the imminence of a danger whereas prevention is a measure or action akin to a hostile danger, though not imminent. 'Prevention can be seen as preemption in slow motion, more anticipatory or forward thinking, perhaps even looking beyond the target's current intentions to those that might develop along with greatly enhanced capacities.'[178] This subtle difference brings another one, in the sense that in prevention, one can decide when to attack and doing so because the opponent remains inferior. As preemption implies the imminence of a threat, one is driven to the wall and thus needs to make an immediate response to a prepared and no more inferior opponent. Preemption therefore is a natural reflex of self-conservation that is much better received than prevention whose aggressive nature is not accepted. That this paradox is not fully understood has provoked great furor amongst quizzical ignoramuses. Another important aspect is the concept of imminence defined as 'something which is 'almost certain to happen very soon'[179] which needs to be reconsidered.

Historical references have been explored in chapter four. Twelve examples of preventive and preemptive attacks have revealed that the only unambiguous case of preemptive war was the victorious Israel's Six Day War of June 1967. The alleged preemptive war against Iraq in 2003 was in fact a preventive one, according to the definitions examined in chapter three.

Chapter five has examined the legal aspects of the concepts of preemption and prevention linked to the principle of anticipatory self-defense. Relating to international law, Article 51 of the UNC authorizes the customary practice of self defense, by using appropriate force, although Article 2(4) prohibits the general use of force. Nevertheless, it seems that there is much divergence of practice and interpretation of Article 51 of the UNC, although whatever right of self defense is to be found in the UNC is customary as well as treaty. Some commentators use the US actions such as in Tripoli, Panama, Iraq, and Afghanistan as 'shifting the Charter paradigm and extending the right of self defense.'[180] Another example extending the right of self defense is the use of preemptive and preventive actions or anticipatory self-defense. Nevertheless, the great majority of other states stay rooted in the narrow conception of self defense.

However nowadays, states prefer to invoke self defense rather than to openly claim anticipatory self defense. This is because the latter is firstly not formally mentioned in the UNC, and secondly is rejected by the vast majority of the states. Moreover, when a state has invoked anticipatory self defense, it has often been condemned by the UNSC and the ICJ. Thus, it can be concluded that the right of preemption and anticipatory self defense is not formally prohibited, but is indeed not well received, although 'few states claim very wide rights of anticipatory self defense to protect nationals, anticipate attack, and to respond to terrorist and other past attacks.'[181] Nonetheless, it is worth stressing that no state can be expected to await the imminence of a threat or an initial attack which, in the present state of armaments, may imperil international stability and security and may well also destroy a state's capacity for further resistance.

The question of whether or not the Third Gulf War was a just war has also been raised. In answering this question, it is important to evaluate it against the seven areas that serve as criteria previously mentioned in chapter six; for a war to be considered just, it must pass a cumulative test. Of course there are many sides of the argument to be considered. However, the spectrum is largely dominated by two main camps: on one end the extreme pacifists, pro-Saddam or even the zealous narrow-minded anti-American detractors are firmly entrenched. Whereas it could be argued that on the other extreme are those who are pro-war or perhaps even erroneously anti-Islam. That is, those who firmly disagree with the action taken against Iraq by the *Coalition of the Willing* are on the left side of the spectrum and those who support this action could be considered right. The former group asserts that the war is unjust basing their foundation on the assumption that the first criteria (just cause) and fourth criteria (legitimate authorities) had not been met. Their position is that there was no backing of the UNSC in March 2003 despite the fact that UN Resolution 1441, passed on November 8th 2002, clearly obliged the Iraqi regime to prove it had disarmed itself of prohibited weapons and the related materials it had not only openly admitted to possessing, but also to those discovered by past inspections. The reality is that Saddam did not comply with this resolution, which subjected him to 'serious consequences'.

Another argument is that no WMD had been found so no war should have been launched. This second assertion is easy to thwart: Iraq is quite a large nation with tremendous amounts of desolate land and underground facilities. This coupled with the fact that Saddam had ample time to adequately hide his WMD arsenal makes for difficult conditions under which the coalition must work to locate them. To further support this argument, one must only turn to the overwhelming number of accurate intelligence reports that provided sufficient evidence to growing international concerns that Saddam was producing and stockpiling WMD against binding UN Resolutions. In addition, the dictator was actively violating human rights, and allegedly had links to terrorist sub-state organisations, such as Al-Qaeda. These reasons and more surely satisfied the criteria for a just war. The situation resulting from the war even now is clearly safer for not only the people of Iraq themselves, who deserve to live in an environment that is free from oppression, but also to the International Community as a whole.

Thus, it is the author's opinion based on the foregoing study that the war in Iraq was justified because it has met the criteria of the just war theory.

Chapter six has assessed the validity of the concepts of pre-emption and prevention by placing them in the spectrum of preventive measures and conflicts. 'When does an armed attack begin to occur? Before soldiers, aircraft or missiles cross the border? From the time that troops are massed or ships set sail?'[182] When a state is supposedly developing WMD and threatening international peace and security? These questions are very controversial and have been subject to heavy debate. Every violation of the territorial integrity or political sovereignty of an independent state is called aggression. Whatever the answer, the requirements of necessity and proportionality should help states to distinguish between reprisals, which are unlawful, and the use of force under Article 51 of the UNC. Moreover, the objective existence of an imminent and real attack, its authentic perception and its use as a pretext for launching military operations should be the preliminary conditions for using force. According to the popular adage 'Prevention is better than a cure,' prevention might be as good a maxim for foreign policy as it is for medicine. The USA assessed the Iraqi threat as imminent, and therefore adopted the better accepted preemptive doctrine. In fact it was preventive, but probably the USA has subtly played on the semantics of both words in the diplomatic arena in order for itself to be perceived as 'a little bit more lawful' than it would have been with prevention. In the real world politics is the art of the possible, and this was strategically perfect.

The vital role of intelligence has also been assessed in this chapter. All the methods of intelligence must be brought to bear against the threat, particularly HUMINT assets. The threat of WMD to US national security is closely linked to the effort to acquire intelligence about terrorism, but WMD collection relies more on TECHINT methodology. The assessment of threats and possible evolutions are a permanent task of intelligence, which has been described in diagram 3.

Further, this chapter addresses the fact that the lethal nature of WMD and 'terrorist assaults [have] led democratic nations to consider the use of retaliation and preemptive military strikes against terrorist bases, training facilities and countries sponsoring terrorism'[183] as well as against CBRN facilities. Thus, the contrasting cases of Iraq and North Korea have also been evaluated to illustrate the strength and weaknesses of the US administration's doctrine of preemption against so-called rogue states. WMD and terrorist organizations remain primary targets of the US NSS but it is also important to point out that human rights' violations may have played an significant role in the decision making process despite the fact that neither the US or UK specifically pointed to them as motivating factors. A persuasive case for this argument can be made by examining the recent historical record: In 1998 NATO attacked Milosevic's Serbia mainly because of human rights' abuses. Despite not having UN backing, the decision is now heralded as having been wholly appropriate. It is critical that the international community consider this and look seriously at such violations in Chechnya, North Korea and Iran. Human rights violations such as mass murders and genocide cannot be left unchecked. They must be dealt with by the international community swiftly and with force if necessary. Hypocrisy cannot reign supreme.

To return to the case of Iraq, it is unfortunate that this argument had not been put forward to the International Community, which had turned its eyes away from the terrible atrocities being committed by Saddam and his regime for more than two decades; it would have likely received greater support than the WMD argument presented to the UN by Colin Powell on February 5th, 2003.

It can be concluded that the new calculus of preemption is another face of the changing security paradigm, but it is one of many means dealing with security like deterrence, preventive diplomacy, and economical measures such as sanctions or incentives. Nevertheless, the record of international crises reveals the need in certain cases to respond rapidly and with force, especially in the case of Iraq. This option should be considered within three basic principles: first, any threat or use of force must be governed by universally accepted principles, as the UN Charter requires. Second the threat or use of force should be regarded as the ultimate resort and third, this option must be part of an integrated, ideally multilateral strategy, and used in conjunction with political and economic instruments.

RECOMMENDATIONS

International law imposes several conditions on the exercise of the right of self defense: first of all, the riposte must be proportionate to the attack, second the SC must intervene *a posteriori*, and third, anticipatory self defense is not well received, although not formally prohibited. If there is no other condition, technological evolution however, has helped renew the juridical reflection on anticipatory self defense. For example; a state positions an armed system in space, to destroy attacking missiles launched from another state. One cannot seriously pretend that this action is a preemptive intervention, because of the characterized attack and the riposte occurring after the aggressor has launched its missiles. Besides, this action is entirely proportionate because its aim is to destroy the missiles. If, from a strategic point of view, it is easy to demonstrate the destabilizing effects of the unilateral installation of these kinds of preventive weapons, the juridical protest is much more delicate according to the relationship between their peaceful use and the UNC. Thus, would it not be conceivable, from then on, to consider the question of anticipatory self defense as a legitimate preventive action reflecting the altruistic aim of future peaceful developments in order to stabilize an insecure situation? Therefore, should this perspective not be observed from the angle of the value that every juridical system is sensible to support? Consequently, anticipatory self-defense could be perceived as the lesser of two evils and so, depending on the circumstances, be formally permitted. If this is the case, an extra article could be introduced in an ideal world where multilateral treaties were capable of being changed through common intelligent consensus. An example of a proposed change to the current UNC might be as follows:

Hypothetical Article 51(2):

'Nothing in the present Charter shall impair the inherent right of individual or collective anticipatory self defense if

a) an imminent armed attack or aggression is likely to occur against a Member of the United Nations and is perceived as such by the majority of the permanent members of the Security Council;

b) a threat of using weapons of mass destruction against a Member of the United Nations endangers the balance of power of the international community;

c) a terrorist threat or imminent attack is likely to occur against a Member of the United Nations; in this case, the operation performed against terrorist organizations must happen without threatening the sovereignty of the state (or only transiently) where these terrorist organizations are located; consent between the involved states about anti-terrorist operations should at least be previously granted, and ideally ratified, as recommended in Resolutions 1269 (1999) and 1368 (2001);

a) the life of nationals abroad is in peril due to an unstable political situation; in this case, the protection or rescue of nationals must be performed without threatening the sovereignty of the state (or only transiently) where nationals are located;

Until the Security Council has taken measures necessary to maintain international peace and security. Measures taken by Members in the exercise of this right of anticipatory self defense shall be immediately reported to the Security Council and shall not in any way affect the authority and responsibility of the Security Council under the present Charter to take at any time such action as it deems necessary in order to maintain or restore international peace and security.'

RECOMMENDATIONS FOR FURTHER RESEARCH

The preceding study has suggested the following areas for further research:

- *There is a need to reconsider the concept of imminence in order to legitimize anticipatory self-defense in the case of preemption.*

- *There is much written advocating the use of intelligence for fighting transnational terrorism. However the use of TE-CHINT has recently proven fruitless in tracking terrorist organizations. HUMINT should be examined more closely and there is a need to train special agents in very specific tasks. Which tasks?*

- *To think the unthinkable by assessing new threats which are not plausible today but may very well be tomorrow.*

OBSERVATIONS

In this author's view the USA can be compared to a Cox or Helmsman in a boat that is transporting some other rowers and friends (allies and partners such as powerful West European countries such as United-Kingdom, France and Germany, and the NATO). The Cox defines the course and should steer its passengers in the right direction. In this regard the Cox has an important guiding / ruling position and some of the passengers may very well dislike the course imposed. Thus, while the USA decides to use preemptive action, it is essential to study the impacts and possible consequences on diplomacy, economy and law with such allies and partners. It is necessary therefore to anticipate the long term effects in order to maintain and improve international relationships. After preemptive action, strategic reconstruction plans with precise defined political objectives need to be defined with allies and partner.

These aspects are suggested to be studied for further research.

Further Personal Considerations

During the development of this work a number of illumina-
tions surfaced regarding the way the geopolitical climate was
changing in the Middle East. While the war was predominate-
ly about the threat Saddam posed to the International Community and to the stability of the Middle East, the USA and its
allies also used it as the catalyst for geopolitical repositioning
that favors those who support democracy in the world. Specifically, in the wake of September 11th, the oppressive Taliban
regime of Afghanistan became the first international pariah
in what may very well be a series, to be forcibly removed in an
effort to increase global security and stability. With the recent
events in Iraq, the geopolitical and strategic repositioning becomes glaringly obvious to those who have a keen perception.
Sandwiched in-between India – long friendly to the UK and
US – and the now allied controlled Afghanistan is the quasi-
friendly but potentially volatile Pakistan. The country's President General Musharaf and his government is an ambiguous,
unstable, fair-weather ally to the West and indeed the Coalition
of the Willing because its allegiances are clearly divided due to
ethnical and religious reasons. Pakistan heavily contributed to
the rise of the Taliban in Afghanistan and moreover was the
only sovereign nation to recognize them diplomatically. These
are issues that most certainly have to be considered in the scope
of global security. In this sense, Afghanistan's geographical
and strategic importance is tremendous. It not only borders
Pakistan but also Iran, which has been a concern of the USA
and its allies for sometime. Prior to the Carter administration,
Iran had been a considerable ally to the USA under the Pahlavi
family. Unfortunately, Carter's characteristic clumsiness and

short-sighted international strategic vision greatly contributed to the fall of the country to the first radical Islamic regime under the control of an Ayatollah Khomeini.[184]

To the North-West of Iran, the USA has strong relations with Turkey and strategic military installations already in place. It is in this context that the control of Iraq begins to complete a puzzle. Directly south of Turkey is Syria. Hafez el-Assad established a bloody dictatorship, which was later assumed by his son Bachar; a man who shares the same characteristics and hatred as his father. With Iraq now cradled in the hands of democracy, Syria is no longer a beneficiary of Saddam's corrupt regime and its misappropriation of Iraqi oil resources and the illegal exportation of weapons. Therefore, Syria's future teeters on a fine line; it must decide their allegiances, cease to shelter and sponsor terrorism, modify its extreme anti-west position, or face 'serious consequences'.

Jordan too, which is the south of Syria and to the west of Iraq is now faced with a harsh reality; their links to Saddam are now broken. Officially a 'pro-west' country, it has 'beaten around the Bush' for far too long; it is important to remember that in 1991 it opposed the US President's action against Iraq. Thus, it is no longer living in the shadow of Saddam and must be more proactive in building positive relations with the USA and its allies.

Saudi Arabia is the center of the Muslim world and an important country in the Middle East. Its importance comes not only from its immense size and wealth, but in the fact that the two holiest cities of the Muslim religion fall within its borders. The reigning family operates within a dangerous dichotomy:

on the one hand they are staunch financiers and supporters of the Wahhabi doctrine; an ultra-strict and austere form of Islam[185] that attracts many of the extremist groups considered to be sub-state terrorist organizations by the USA and its allies. 'While Islam and Islamism are two different things, the border separating these two notions is porous.'[186] But on the other hand, they claim overtly to be themselves allies of the West and entertain western culture, give to western universities, invest in western businesses, and enjoy opulent western lifestyles – all the while neglecting their own people. Saudis who are not privileged at birth or do not benefit from commercial and personal relationships developed with the royal family live in substandard conditions in underdeveloped communities.

The fall of Iraq with its considerable resources and the fact that it borders the nations mentioned above, makes it the ideal strategic location to forward western concepts of democracy and to establish mechanisms – both political and military – for counter-balancing threats to democratic allies such as Israel and to global security that may emerge in the future from the Middle East.

The reality is we live in a world with a single super power: the United States of America. While its actions are often not well received by too timid members of the International Community, it possesses the intestinal fortitude to do the things that others do not dare: to take action and initiative in order to assist in the security and peace of our world. As President Bush put it, America has the duty 'to fight not to impose [its] will, but to defend [itself] and extend the blessings of freedom.'[187]

DESSERT

Salade d'oranges

Finally, as you find yourself full and sitting comfortably from the previous dishes, it is time to enjoy a delicate bowl of sweet fruit. Simple in preparation and presentation, it lacks nothing in taste!

Please now turn briefly to the final photograph located in the center of the book. Remember also that these recipes and more can be found at ***www.wonderfood.biz*** and of course my own website ***www.ericklabara.com***.

"He who stays on the defensive does not make war, he endures it."

Field Marshal Colmar Baron von der Goltz, 1883

AUTHOR'S NOTE

This is the only time anywhere in this book that I have taken the liberty to address you – *the reader* – on a personal level. The reason for this is because my intentions were to provide a reasonably unbiased analysis of pressing issues that affect us greatly today without delving too much into my own views; it is important that you are able to reach your own conclusions.

As a Swiss military officer I have diverged in large part from my own country's dominant political and military views. It is important that I point out that my views are my own and do not represent the Swiss government or Swiss armed forces.

The culinary, or rather gastronomic, diversions were intended to add something different and special to the book; they are a presentation of my ideas on what are of value when it comes to enjoying good meals — an issue that all of us can relate to as human beings regardless of the political climate we find ourselves in.

Along with the assistance of Richard Holmes, Christopher Bellamy, James L. Clark, Global Security Press, and countless others, it has been my sincere pleasure to bring to you this unique mixture; I hope you have enjoyed reading it as much as I enjoyed writing it for you.

Erick Labara
www.ericklabara.com

APPENDIX A-1

IRAQ'S WMD Delivery Systems

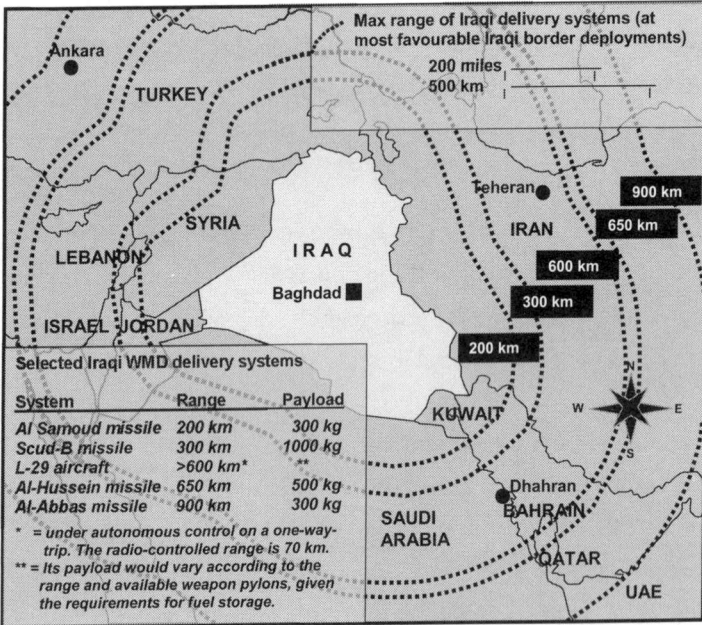

Source: http://www.iiss.org/showfullimageg.php?imgID=47&galleryID=4

APPENDIX A-2

Key Iraqi Nuclear Weapons Sites (1990-2002)

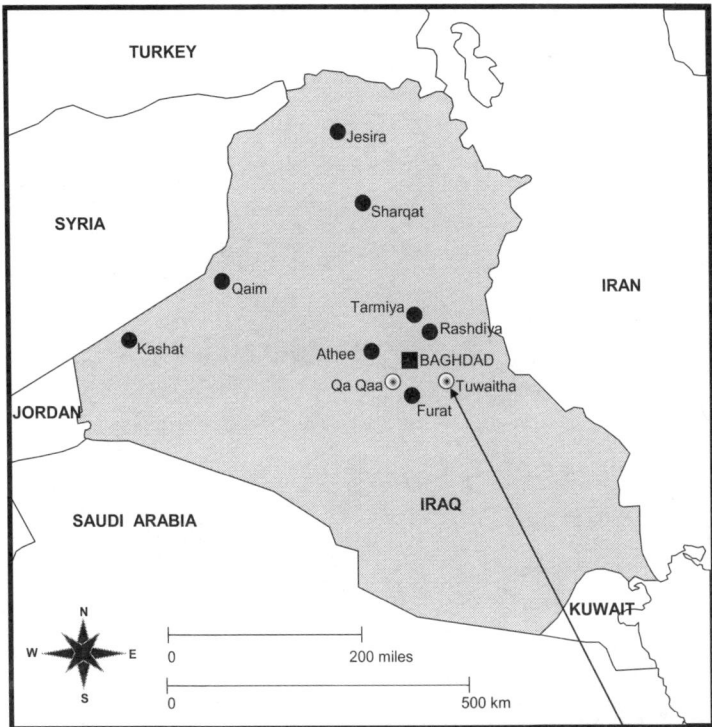

TURKEY

Jesira

Sharqat

SYRIA

Qaim

Tarmiya
Rashdiya

Kashat

Athee
BAGHDAD

Qa Qaa
Tuwaitha

JORDAN

Furat

IRAN

IRAQ

SAUDI ARABIA

KUWAIT

N
W E
S

0
200 miles

0
500 km

LEGEND

● Destroyed or inactive (1991–98)

⊛ Active in civilian or non-proscribed military activities (UN monitored until December 1998)

Iraqi nuclear reactor attacked by Israeli forces in 1981

This map depicts major facilities for the production of fissile material and weaponisation. If Iraq acquired usable nuclear material, construction of a nuclear device could take place at other locations.

Source: http://www.iiss.org/showfullimageg.php?imgID=49&galleryID=4

APPENDIX A-3

Key Iraqi Biological Weapons Sites (1990-2002)

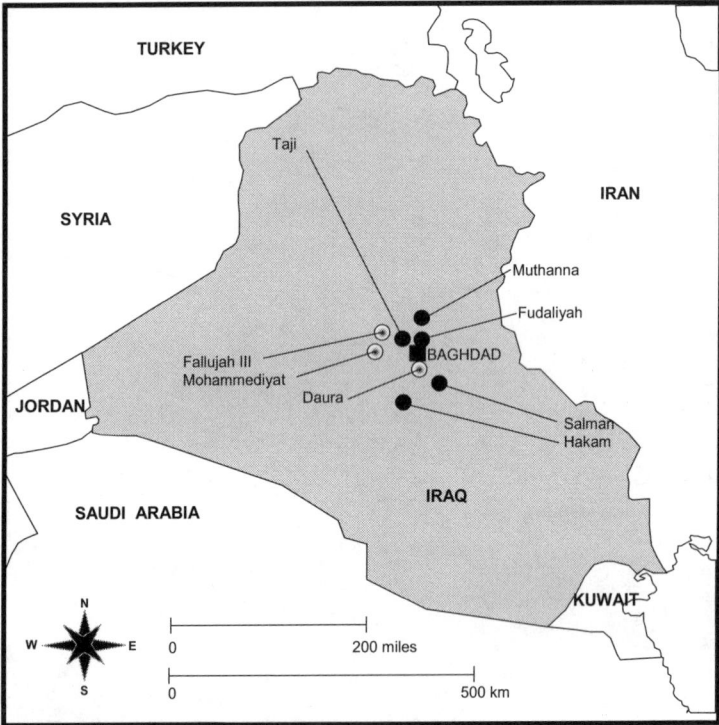

LEGEND

● Destroyed or inactive (1991–98)

⊛ Active in civilian or non-proscribed military activities (UN monitored until December 1998)

This map does not depict possible covert biological weapons facilities or civilian dual use facilities that could have been requisitioned for offensive biological weapons program.

Source: http://www.iiss.org/showfullimageg.php?imgID=44&galleryID=4

APPENDIX A-4

Key Iraqi Chemical Weapons Sites (1990-2002)

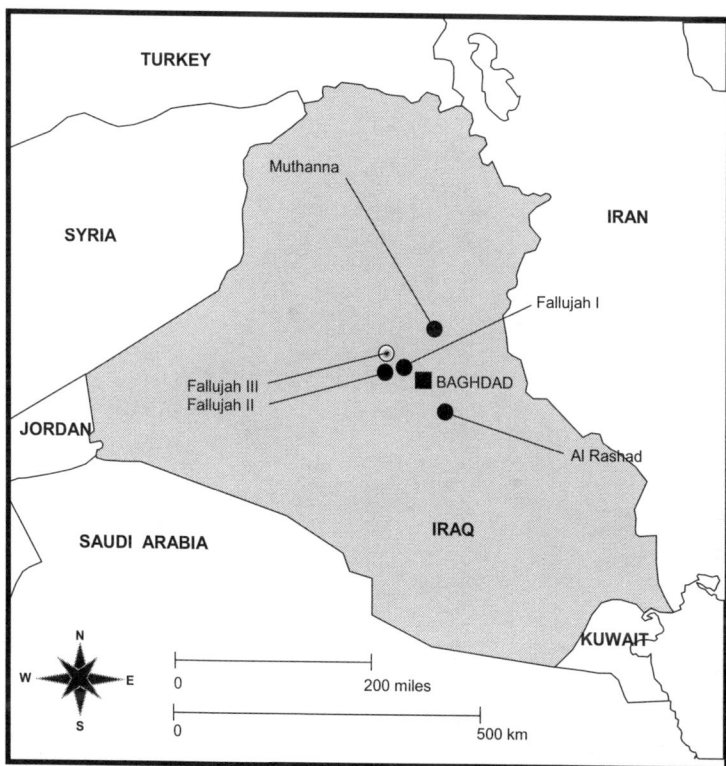

LEGEND

● Destroyed or inactive (1991–98)

⊛ Active in civilian or non-proscribed military activities (UN monitored until December 1998)

This map does not depict possible covert chemical weapons facilities or civilian dual use facilities that could have been requisitioned for offensive chemical weapons program.

Source: http://www.iiss.org/showfullimageg.php?imgID=45&galleryID=4

APPENDIX A-5

Key Iraqi Balistic Missle Sites (1990-2002)

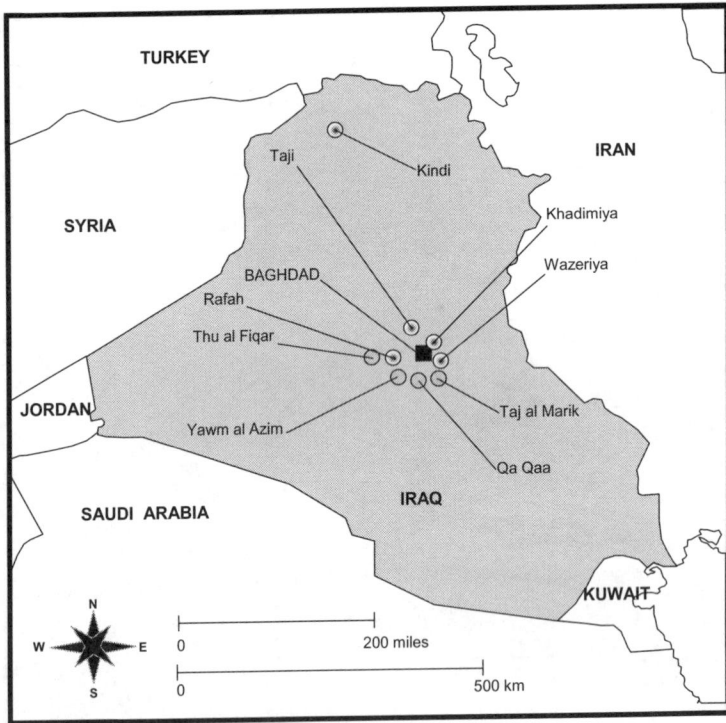

LEGEND

⊘ Active in civilian or non-proscribed
military activities (UN monitored until
December 1998)

⊛ Active in permitted missile programs,
targeted in 1998, some reportedly rebuilt

*This map does not depict any possible
covert ballistic missile facilities or
facilities involved in permitted missile
activities that have not been made
public.*

ERICK LABARA

APPENDIX B

IRAQ'S WEAPONS OF MASS DESTRUCTION, THE ASSESSMENT OF THE BRITISH GOVERNMENT

EXECUTIVE SUMMARY

1. Under Saddam Hussein Iraq developed chemical and biological weapons, acquired missiles allowing it to attack neighboring countries with these weapons and persistently tried to develop a nuclear bomb. Saddam has used chemical weapons, both against Iran and against his own people. Following the Gulf War, Iraq had to admit to all this. And in the ceasefire of 1991 Saddam agreed unconditionally to give up his weapons of mass destruction.

2. Much information about Iraq's weapons of mass destruction is already in the public domain from UN reports and from Iraqi defectors. This clearly points to Iraq's continuing possession, after 1991, of chemical and biological agents and weapons produced before the Gulf War. It shows that Iraq has refurbished sites formerly associated with the production of chemical and biological agents. And it indicates that Iraq remains able to manufacture these agents, and to use bombs, shells, artillery rockets and ballistic missiles to deliver them.

3. An independent and well-researched overview of this public evidence was provided by the International Institute for Strategic Studies (IISS) on 9 September. The IISS report also suggested that Iraq could assemble nuclear weapons within months of obtaining fissile

material from foreign sources.

4. As well as the public evidence, however, significant additional information is available to the Government from secret intelligence sources, described in more detail in this paper. This intelligence cannot tell us about everything. However, it provides a fuller picture of Iraqi plans and capabilities. It shows that Saddam Hussein attaches great importance to possessing weapons of mass destruction which he regards as the basis for Iraq's regional power. It shows that he does not regard them only as weapons of last resort. He is ready to use them, including against his own population, and is determined to retain them, in breach of United Nations Security Council Resolutions (UNSCR).

5. Intelligence also shows that Iraq is preparing plans to conceal evidence of these weapons, including incriminating documents, from renewed inspections. And it confirms that despite sanctions and the policy of containment, Saddam has continued to make progress with his illicit weapons programs.

6. As a result of the intelligence we judge that Iraq has:

- *continued to produce chemical and biological agents;*

- *military plans for the use of chemical and biological weapons, including against its own Shia population. Some of these weapons are deployable within 45 minutes of an order to use them;*

- *command and control arrangements in place to use chemical and biological weapons. Authority ultimately resides with Saddam Hussein. (There is intelligence that he may have delegated this authority to his son Qusai);*

- *developed mobile laboratories for military use, corroborat-*

ing earlier reports about the mobile production of biological
warfare agents;

• pursued illegal programmes to procure controlled materials
of potential use in the production of chemical and biological
weapons programmes;

• tried covertly to acquire technology and materials which
could be used in the production of nuclear weapons;

• sought significant quantities of uranium from Africa, despite having no active civil nuclear power programme that
could require it;

• recalled specialists to work on its nuclear programme;

• illegally retained up to 20 al-Hussein missiles, with a range
of 650km, capable of carrying chemical or biological war-
heads;

• started deploying its al-Samoud liquid propellant missile,
and has used the absence of weapons inspectors to work on
extending its range to at least 200km, which is beyond the
limit of 150km imposed by the United Nations;

• started producing the solid-propellant Ababil-100, and is
making efforts to extend its range to at least 200km, which is
beyond the limit of 150km imposed by the United Nations;

• constructed a new engine test stand for the development of
missiles capable of reaching the UK Sovereign Base Areas in
Cyprus and NATO members (Greece and Turkey), as well as
all Iraq's Gulf neighbours and Israel;

• pursued illegal programmes to procure materials for use in
its illegal development of long range missiles;

• learnt lessons from previous UN weapons inspections and
has already begun to conceal sensitive equipment and documentation in advance of the return of inspectors.

7. These judgments reflect the views of the Joint Intelligence Committee (JIC). More details on the judgments and on the development of the JIC's assessments since 1998 are set out in Part 1 of this paper.

8. Iraq's weapons of mass destruction are in breach of international law. Under a series of UN Security Council Resolutions Iraq is obliged to destroy its holdings of these weapons under the supervision of UN inspectors. Part 2 of the paper sets out the key UN Security Council Resolutions. It also summarises the history of the UN inspection regime and Iraq's history of deception, intimidation and concealment in its dealings with the UN inspectors.

9. But the threat from Iraq does not depend solely on the capabilities we have described. It arises also because of the violent and aggressive nature of Saddam Hussein's regime. His record of internal repression and external aggression gives rise to unique concerns about the threat he poses. The paper briefly outlines in Part 3 Saddam's rise to power, the nature of his regime and his history of regional aggression. Saddam's human rights abuses are also catalogued, including his record of torture, mass arrests and summary executions.

10. The paper briefly sets out how Iraq is able to finance its weapons programme. Drawing on illicit earnings generated outside UN control, Iraq generated illegal income of some $3 billion in 2001.

BIBLIOGRAPHY

BOOKS AND MONOGRAPHS

Arquilla, John, *Dubious Battles, Aggression, Defeat, and the International System*, RAND, Library of Congress Cataloging-in-Publication Data, USA, 1992.

Bachofner, Hans, *Versäumte Chancen, Sicherheitspolitik nach dem 11. September 2001*, Schweizerzeit-Schriftenreihe Nr. 40, Schweizerzeit Verlags AG, 8416 Flaach, Switzerland, April 2002.

Baud, Jacques, *La Guerre Assymétrique ou la Défaite du Vainqueur*, L'Art de la Guerre, Editions du Rocher, Paris, 2003.

Clausewitz, Carl von, *On War*, (*Vom Kriege*, 1832) translated by Michael Howard and Peter Paret, Princeton University Press, Princeton NJ, 1976.

Fontaine, Jean de la, *Fables*, Ed. J. Dupuis Fils & Co, Marcinelle-Charleroi, Belgique, 1970.

Gray, Christine, *International Law and the Use of Force*, Oxford University Press Inc., New York, 2000.

Hamburg, David A. and Vance, Cyrus R., *Preventing Deadly Conflicts*, Carnegie Corporation of New York, 1997.

Harris, D.J., *Cases and Materials on International Law*, Sweet and Maxwell Limited, London, 1998.

Hippo, St. Augustine of, *Against Faustus the Manichaean*, in Augustine: Political Writings, translated by Michael W. Tkacz and Douglas Kries, Ed. Ernest L. Fortin and Douglas Kries, USA, 1994.

Hughes-Wilson, John, *Military Intelligence Blunders*, Constable Publishers, London, 1999.

Johnson, James Turner, *Just War Tradition and Low-Intensity Conflict*, in Legal and Moral Constraints on Low-Intensity Conflict, Alberto R. Coll, et al. Editors, USA, 1995.

Knight, Ian and Castle, Ian, *The Zulu War Then and Now*, Plaistow Press Ltd, London, 1993.

McBride, Angus, *The Zulu War*, Osprey Publishing Ltd, London, 1976.

Mougenot, Pierre, *Atlas Historique*, Librairie Stock, Paris, 1968.

Nye, Joseph S., Jr, *Understanding International Conflicts, An Introduction to Theory and History*, Longman, Library of Congress Cataloging-in-Publication Data, USA, 2000.

O'Brien, William V., *Just War Doctrine's Complementary Role in the International Law of War*, in Legal and Moral Constraints on Low-Intensity Conflict, Alberto R. Coll, et al. Editors, USA, 1995.

Poland, James M., *Understanding Terrorism, Groups, Strategies and Responses*, Prentice-Hall, Inc., New Jersey, USA, 1988

Roberts, Adam and Guelff, Richard, *Documents on the Law of Wars*, 3rd Edition, Oxford University Press, 2000.

Rotbeg, Robert I. and Rabb, Theodore K., *The Origin and Preven-*

tion of Major Wars, Press Syndicate of the University of Cambridge, 1988.

Sarooshi, Danesh, *The United Nations and the Development of Collective Security: The Delegation by the UN Security Council of its Chapter VII Powers*, Oxford University Press Inc., New York, 1999.

Thucydides, *La Guerre du Péloponèse*, Volume 1, Book 1, XXXI to LII, translated by Jacqueline de Romilly, Ed. Belles Lettres, Paris, 1981.

Tzu, Sun, *The Art of War*, translated by Samuel B. Griffith, Oxford University Press, UK, 1963.

Walzer, Michael, *Just and Unjust Wars*, Basic Books, Third Edition, New York, 2000.

Whittaker, David J., *The Terrorism Reader*, 2nd Edition, Routledge, London, 2003.

Williams, Paul L., *Al Qaeda, Brotherhood of Terror*, Alpha, A Pearson Education Company, USA, 2002.

DICTIONARIES

_____, Cobuild, *English Dictionary for Advanced Learners*, 3rd Edition, Harper Collins Publishers, Glasgow, 2001.

_____, *The New Shorter Oxford English Dictionary on Historical Principles*, 4th Edition, Vol. 2, Oxford University Press, 1993.

_____, *Webster's Ninth New Collegiate Dictionary*, Merriam-Webster Inc., Publishers, Springfield, Massachusetts, USA,

1987.

_____, *US Department of Defence's Dictionary on Military Terms*, US Department of Defence, USA, 2002.

OFFICIAL REPORTS (SEE ALSO INTERNET SOURCES)

_____, *Iraq's Weapons of Mass Destruction, The Assessment of the British Government*, The Stationery Office Limited, London, 2002

The White House, *A National Strategy for a New Century*, The White House, December 1999.

The White House, *National Security Strategy of the United States of America*, The White House, September 17th 2002.

CONFERENCES

The author attended a number of conferences from which he gained invaluable information, including:

- *Global Security Conference, October 9th - 10th 2002 at Shrivenham, on the themes of Terrorism, National Resilience, Conflict Prevention and Disaster and Risk Management*
- *First Cranfield University International Conference on Defence Management, April 24th and 25th 2003 at Oxford Belfry, on the theme of Post-Modern Military: Rethinking the Future*

ARTICLES

Bederman, David J., *Reception of the Classical Tradition in International Law: Grotius' De Jure Belli Ac Pacis*, Emory International Law Review, Volume 10, USA, Spring 1996.

Haines, Steven, *Military Intervention and International Law*, in Trevor Salmon, Ed., Issues in International Politics, Routeledge, London, 2000.

Hoffman, Bruce, *Old Madness, New Methods*, Rand Review Winter 1998-99, USA, 1999.

Johnson, Loch K., *Secret Agencies: U.S. Intelligence in a Hostile World*, Yale University Press, 1996.

Litwak, Robert S., *The New Calculus of Pre-emption*, in Survival, Volume 44, Number 4, Winter 2002-03, The International Institute for Strategic Studies, 2002.

Nesmith, Jeff, *US Satellite Eavesdroppers Seek Needles in Global Haystack*, Cox News, Washington Bureau, 7.10.2001.

Slocombe, Walter B., *Force, Pre-emption and Legitimacy*, in Survival, The IISS Quarterly, Volume 45, Number 1, The International Institute for Strategic studies, Spring 2003.

_____, *The United States: Changed Utterly?*, in Strategic Survey 2002/2003, The International Institute for Strategic Studies, Oxford University Press, May 2003.

_____, *US and the Middle East After 11 September*, in Strategic Survey 2001/2002, The International Institute for Strategic Studies, Oxford University Press, 2002.

INTERNET SOURCES

Amnesty International's 10-point appeal. See Web site:

http://www.amnesty.org.nz/web/Pages/home.nsf/dd5cab6801f1
723585256474005327c8/d04e52d0f0188875cc256d1d001e2b89!O
penDocument

Aquinas, Thomas, *Summa Theologica II-II*, Question 40, 'On
War', Article 1; See also Web Site: http://eawc.evansville.edu/an-
thology/aquinas40.htm

Confucius, see website: http://perso.wanadoo.fr/marc.vanderme/
aphorismes.htm

DeForrest, Mark Edward, *Just War Theory and the Recent U.S.
Air Strikes against Iraq*, See Website: http://law.gonzaga.edu/or-
ders/documents/deforrest.htm#INTRODUCTION

Freedman, Lawrence, *Prevention, Not Pre-emption*, in The Washington Quarterly, (Spring 2003) Web site: http://www.twq.com/
03spring/docs/03spring_freedman.pdf

Hawking, Stephen, http://healthwriting.com/quotes.htm

Hoffman, Bruce, *Old Madness, New Methods*, Rand Review Winter 1998-99. 29.9.2002. Web Site: http://www.rand.org/publica-
tions/randreview/issues/rrwinter98.9.pdf

Kissinger, Henry, *Why is Henry Kissinger interpreted in so many
ways?*, ParaPundit.com, 12.9.2002. Web Site: http://www.para-
pundit.com/archives/000053.html

Kroening, Volker, *Prevention or Pre-emption? - Towards a Clarification of Terminology*. Web site: http://www.basicint.org/iraq-
conflict/Pubs/Web%20Notes/WN180303.htm

Nesmith, Jeff, *US Satellite Eavesdroppers Seek Needles in Global Haystack*, Cox News, Washington Bureau, 7.10.2001 and 29.9.2002. Web site: http://www.coxnews.com/washingtonbureau/staff/nesmith/100701TER-ECHELON.html

Patton, George, General, http://www.cs.virginia.edu/~robins/quotes.html

Twain Mark, http://www.cs.virginia.edu/~robins/quotes.html

UN RESOLUTIONS

UN Resolution 660 (August 2nd 1990): http://ods-dds-ny.un.org/doc/RESOLUTION/GEN/NR0/575/10/IMG/NR057510.pdf?OpenElement

UN Resolution 678 (November 29th 1990): http://ods-dds-ny.un.org/doc/RESOLUTION/GEN/NR0/575/28/IMG/NR057528.pdf?OpenElement

UN Resolution 1373 (September 28th 2001): http://ods-dds-ny.un.org/doc/UNDOC/GEN/N01/557/43/PDF/N0155743.pdf?OpenElement

UN Resolution 1441 (November 8th 2002): http://ods-dds-ny.un.org/doc/UNDOC/GEN/N02/682/26/PDF/N0268226.pdf?OpenElement

WHITE HOUSE WEB SITES

President's State of the Union address, January 29th 2002: http://www.whitehouse.gov/news/releases/2002/01/20020129-11.html

President's Graduation Speech at West Point, June 1st 2002: http://www.whitehouse.gov/news/releases/2002/06/20020601-3.html

The National Security Strategy of the United States of America, see US NSS document: http://www.whitehouse.gov/nsc/nss.html

Chapter 5 of the US NSS: http://www.whitehouse.gov/nsc/nss5.html

MAPS

Iraq's WMD Delivery Systems: http://www.iiss.org/showfullimageg.php?imgID=47&galleryID=4

Key Iraqi Nuclear Sites (1990-2002): http://www.iiss.org/showfullimageg.php?imgID=49&galleryID=4

Key Iraqi Biological Weapons Sites (1990-2002): http://www.iiss.org/showfullimageg.php?imgID=44&galleryID=4

Key Iraqi Chemical Weapons Sites (1990-2002): http://www.iiss.org/showfullimageg.php?imgID=45&galleryID=4

Key Iraqi Ballistic Missile Sites (1990-2002): http://www.iiss.org/showfullimageg.php?imgID=48&galleryID=4

PICTURES (NOT IN THE BOOK)

Yongbyon's North Korean Nuclear Reactor (March 5th 2003) http://www.globalsecurity.org/wmd/world/dprk/yongbyon-imagery.htm

REFERENCES

1. Sen. John Kerry As Quoted On NPR's "All Things Considered," 3/19/03

CHAPTER ONE

2. Thucydides, *La Guerre du Péloponèse*, Volume 1, Book 1, XXXI to LII, translated by Jacqueline de Romilly, (Ed. Belles Lettres, Paris, 1981), p. 247

3. White House Web site: http://www.whitehouse.gov/news/releases/2002/06/20020601-3.html

4. WMD are also called 'CBRN' weapons, which means Chemical, Biological, Radiological and Nuclear

5. Robert S. Litwak, *The New Calculus of Pre-emption*, in Survival, Volume 44, Number 4, Winter 2002-2003, (The International Institute for Strategic Studies, 2002), p. 53

6. Ibid., p. 53

7. On August 2nd and on the 4th, 1964, the North Vietnamese torpedo-boats attacked US warships in the Gulf of Tonkin. In retaliation, on August 5 1964, the US bombed the base from which the torpedo-boats operated and an oil storage depot to great effect. D.J. Harris, *Cases and Materials on International Law*, (Sweet and Maxwell Limited, London, 1998), p. 901

8. Ibid., p. 898

9. One of the missions of the DTRA after September 11th 2001 was to come up with a device that could penetrate Al Qaeda's cave complexes in the mountains of Afghanistan and kill the people inside.

10. Henry Kissinger, *Why is Henry Kissinger interpreted in so many ways?*, (ParaPundit.com, 12.9.2002), Web Site: http://www.parapundit.com/archives/000053.html

11. Resolution 1441 asks the Iraqi regime to prove that it has disarmed by accounting for proscribed weapons and materials that it was found to possess through past inspections and by its own admissions. See also UN Web site: http://ods-dds-ny.un.org/doc/UNDOC/GEN/N02/682/26/PDF/N0268226.pdf?OpenElement

12. 'When the United Nations named Hans Blix as the chief weapons inspector, it, as been said, chose a flock of fowls to hunt the fox. Blix's record strongly suggests that he was far too cautious, too respectful of Iraq's official pronouncements, and entirely too concerned with diplomatic niceties to carry out the kind of forceful inspections needed by the international community to disarm Iraq.' (Source Unknown)

13. The Monroe Doctrine was expressed during President Monroe's seventh annual message to Congress, December 2, 1823. Essentially, the United States was informing the powers of the Old World that the American continents were no longer open to European colonisation, and that any effort to extend European political influence into the New World would be considered by the United States as dangerous to our peace and safety.' The United States would not interfere in European wars or internal affairs, and expected Europe to stay out of American affairs.

14. Henry Kissinger, op. cit., Web Site: http://www.parapundit.com/archives/000053.html

CHAPTER TWO

15. Mark Twain, http://www.cs.virginia.edu/~robins/quotes.html

16. http://www.google.com/

CHAPTER THREE

17. Stephen Hawking, http://healthwriting.com/quotes.htm

18. _____, *Webster's Ninth New Collegiate Dictionary*, (Merriam-Webster Inc., Publishers, Springfield, Massachusetts, USA, 1987), p. 927

19. Ibid., p. 927

20. _____, *Cobuild, English Dictionary for Advanced Learners*, (3rd Edition, Harper Collins Publishers, Glasgow, 2001), p. 1206

21. Ibid., p. 1206

22. _____, *The New Shorter Oxford English Dictionary on Historical Principles*, (4th Edition, Vol. 2, Oxford University Press, 1993), p. 2330

23. Ibid., p. 2330

24. Volker Kroening, *Prevention or Pre-emption?* - Towards a Clarification of Terminology, Web site: http://www.basicint.org/iraqconflict/Pubs/Web%20Notes/WN180303.htm, p. 1

25. *Webster's Ninth New Collegiate Dictionary*, op. cit., p. 933

26. Ibid., p. 933

27. *Cobuild, English Dictionary for Advanced Learners*, op. cit., p. 1214

28. *The New Shorter Oxford English Dictionary on Historical Principles*, op. cit., p. 2348

29. *Webster's Ninth New Collegiate Dictionary*, op. cit., p. 933

30. *Cobuild, English Dictionary for Advanced Learners*, op. cit.,

p. 1214

31. *The New Shorter Oxford English Dictionary on Historical Principles*, op. cit., p. 2348

32. Ibid., p. 2348

33. Volker Kroening, op. cit., p. 1

34. Lawrence Freedman, *Prevention, Not Pre-emption*, in The Washington Quarterly, (Spring 2003) Web site: http://www.twq.com/03spring/docs/03spring_freedman.pdf, p. 106

35. Joseph S. Nye, Jr, *Understanding International Conflicts, An Introduction to Theory and History*, (Longman, Library of Congress Cataloging-in-Publication Data, USA, 2000), p. 151

36. Lawrence Freedman, op. cit., p. 106

37. Ibid., p. 106

38. Robert S. Litwak, op. cit., p. 67

39. Lawrence Freedman, op. cit., p. 106

40. *Cobuild, English Dictionary for Advanced Learners*, op. cit., p. 781

41. Lawrence Freedman, op. cit., p. 113

42. There is some controversy about the numeric denomination of the Gulf Wars. Some argue that there were two, others say three. In this dissertation, we will speak of three Gulf Wars; Indeed, Gulf War I was the Iran-Iraq War (1980 - 1988), Gulf War II, the US led War against Iraq in 1991 and Gulf War III the latest which occurred in 2003.

CHAPTER FOUR

43. Confucius, http://perso.wanadoo.fr/marc.vanderme/aphorismes.htm

44. D.J. Harris, op. cit., p. 894

45. Ibid., p. 894

46. Ian Knight and Ian Castle, *The Zulu War Then and Now*, (Plaistow Press Ltd, London, 1993), p. 13

47. Ibid., p. 13

48. Ibid., p. 14

49. Ibid., p. 12

50. An excellent book to read on this subject is called '*The Zulu War*' by Angus McBride, (Osprey Publishing Ltd, London, 1976)

51. Ibid., p. 15

52. Ibid., p. 14

53. Ian Knight and Ian Castle, op. cit., p. 14

54. Ibid., p. 15

55. Pierre Mougenot, *Atlas Historique*, (Librairie Stock, Paris, 1968), pp. 449 and 493

56. Michael Walzer, *Just and Unjust Wars*, (Basic Books, Third Edition, New York, 2000), p. 82

57. Christine Gray, op. cit., p. 113

58. Ibid., p. 100

59. D.J. Harris, op. cit., pp. 440-443

60. Ibid., pp. 840, 843-844

61. Ibid, p. 866

62. The Black Legend was created in Elizabethan England as a way to arouse nationalistic sentiment against the Spanish Armada. Oliver Cromwell fortified it with vicious racial and religious attacks against the Spanish character.

63. Just war theory has a varied and diverse background. The just war tradition includes the contributions of philosophers and theologians dating back to Roman times. As James Tuner Johnson has pointed out, Just war is an historical tradition formed by experience and reflection, including much that is neither specifically theological, (nor even religious) nor philosophical. It has been strongly influenced by international law, the traditions of chivalry, and soldierly practices derived from the experience of many battles. Just war theory as a method of evaluating military actions has been recognized historically by thinkers as varied as Cicero, St. Augustine, St. Thomas Aquinas, Grotius, and Daniel Webster. It is a theory which has been used by Christians and non-Christians alike to determine whether or not the decision to go to war and the means used to prosecute that war are just.

64. Robert S. Litwak, op. cit., p. 67

65. D.J. Harris, op. cit., p. 898

66. Robert S. Litwak, op. cit., p. 65

67. Ibid., p. 66

68. *Realpolitik* or the power politics is the major feature of the Realists' ideology. For the Realists, the main actors in international relations are states, which act in their national interests. These are defined only in terms of power (supreme authority

domestically and independence internationally). The Realist view of international politics is a state of war of all against all. In the Realist tradition, the principal governing considerations of foreign policy are military and economic strength, geographical location and the balance of power, whereby states act so as to prevent any one state dominating. This notion was observed and has been maintained, in some form or other, by every US President up to George Bush Sr and nowadays by George W. Bush Jr. Other illustrious figures representing Realism were Thucydides (460- 406 BC), Niccolo Machiavelli (1469-1527), Thomas Hobbes (1588-1679) and Jean-Jacques Rousseau (1712-78).

69. David J. Whittaker, *The Terrorism Reader*, (2nd Edition, Routledge, London, 2003), p. 41

70. Paul L. Williams, *Al Qaeda, Brotherhood of Terror*, (Alpha, A Pearson Education Company, USA, 2002), p. 82

71. Lawrence Freedman, op. cit., p. 112

72. Ibid., pp. 113-114

73. Ibid., p. 114

74. See note 41

75. On December 20th 1989, the USA invaded Panama, sending troops to supplement others already based there, to overthrow the government of General Noriega. After some resistance by Noriega's forces, the invasion was successful, with General Noriega surrendering to the US authorities, after initially taking refuge in the papal nuncio's residence. He was then flown to the USA to face drugs charges. See also D.J. Harris, op. cit., pp. 893-894

76. _____, *US and the Middle East After 11 September*, in Strategic Survey 2001/2002, The International Institute for Strategic Studies, (Oxford University Press, 2002), p. 179

77. _____, *US and the Middle East After 11 September*, in Strategic Survey 2001/2002, op. cit., p. 188

78. Robert S. Litwak, op.cit., p. 54

79. Ibid., p. 54

80. _____, *The United States: Changed Utterly?*, in Strategic Survey 2002/2003, The International Institute for Strategic Studies, (Oxford University Press, May 2003), p. 69

81. Lawrence Freedman, op. cit., p. 112

82. John Arquilla, *Dubious Battles, Aggression, Defeat, and the International System*, (RAND, Library of Congress Cataloging-in-Publication Data,USA, 1992), p. 14

CHAPTER FIVE

83. St. Augustine of Hippo, *Against Faustus the Manichaean*, in Augustine: Political Writings, (translated by Michael W. Tkacz and Douglas Kries, Ed. Ernest L. Fortin and Douglas Kries, USA, 1994), p. 220

84. D.J. Harris, op. cit., p. 1049

85. Steven Haines, *Military Intervention and International Law*, in Trevor Salmon, Ed., Issues in International Politics, (Routeledge, London, 2000), pp. 100-129

86. Christine Gray, *International Law and the Use of Force*, (Oxford University Press Inc., New York, 2000), p. 84

87. Article 5 NATO (parts): 'The Parties agree that an armed attack against one or more of them ... shall be considered an attack against them all; and consequently they agree that if such an armed attack occurs, each of them in the exercise of the right of individual or collective self defence recognised in Article 51 of the Charter of the United Nations ... [will take] ...

such action as it deems necessary, including the use of armed force, to secure and maintain the security of the North Atlantic area.'

88. D.J. Harris, op. cit., p. 1060

89. In the French text of the UN Charter, the term 'armed attack' is translated by 'aggression armée' (armed aggression) which provokes a doctrinal conflict. In international law, the notion of 'aggression' has a particular connotation; indeed, it assumes different characteristics with various degrees. A definition of this notion has been given on December 14th 1974 in the Resolution 3314 (XXIX), art. 1, vol. I, p. 258.

90. Christine Gray, op. cit., pp. 120-143 and Danesh Sarooshi, *The United Nations and the Development of Collective Security: The Delegation by the UN Security Council of its Chapter VII Powers*, (Oxford University Press Inc., New York, 1999), pp. 200-207

91. D.J. Harris, op. cit., p. 1056

92. Ibid., p. 1058

93. Adam Roberts and Richard Guelff, *Documents on the Law of Wars*, (3rd Edition, Oxford University Press, 2000), pp. 10, 575, 593

94. D.J. Harris, op. cit., p. 894

95. Ibid., p. 896

96. Ibid., p. 866

97. The ICJ is the court which statues about the outcomes of disputes between states, but not between people. At international level, disputes between people are settled by the International Criminal Court (ICC).

98. D.J. Harris, op. cit., pp. 872-873

99. Christine Gray, op. cit., p. 119

100. Michael Walzer, op. cit., p. 75

101. Christine Gray, op. cit., pp. 111-112

102. D.J. Harris, op. cit., p. 897

103. Ibid., p. 897

104. Christine Gray, op. cit., p. 119

105. James Turner Johnson, *Just War Tradition and Low-Intensity Conflict, in Legal and Moral Constraints on Low-Intensity Conflict*, (Alberto R. Coll et al. Editors, USA, 1995), p. 148

106. Hugo Grotius (1583-1645) was known as the father of international law. His most recognized work which gave him this title was his 1625 masterpiece - *De Jure Belle ac Pacis*: On the Law of War and Peace; Hugo Grotius, *De Jure Belli ac Pacis* (1646 ed., F.W. Kelsey et al, trans., 1964)

107. Mark Edward DeForrest, *Just War Theory and the Recent U.S. Air Strikes against Iraq*, See Web Site: http://law.gonzaga.edu/borders/documents/deforres.htm#INTRODUCTION

108. Mark Edward DeForrest, Ibid.; See also David J. Bederman, *Reception of the Classical Tradition in International Law: Grotius' De Jure Belli Ac Pacis*, (Emory International Law Review, Volume 10, USA, Spring 1996), p. 29;

109. Mark Edward DeForrest, Ibid.; See also James Turner Johnson, op. cit., p. 149

110. Mark Edward DeForrest, Ibid.; See also James Turner Johnson, Ibid.

111. See following Web Sites (non-exhaustive list):

http://byzantinecalvinist.blogspot.com/2003_10_01_byzantinecalvinist_archive.html

http://www.soci.niu.edu/~phildept/Kapitan/JW1.html

http://www.utm.edu/research/iep/j/justwar.htm

http://www.aclj.org/news/bibpers/020917_preemptive.asp

112. See Web Site: http://www.yale.edu/lawweb/avalon/lawofwar/lawwar.htm

113. See Web Site: http://www.wand.org/9-11/justwar.html

114. William V. O'Brien, *Just War Doctrine's Complementary Role in the International Law of War*, in Legal and Moral Constraints on Low-Intensity Conflict, (Alberto R. coll, et al. Editors, USA, 1995), p. 181

115. Ibid., p. 191

116. See Web Site: http://www.wand.org/9-11/justwar.html

117. Thomas Aquinas, *Summa Theologica II-II*, Question 40, 'On War', Article 1; See also Web Site: http://eawc.evansville.edu/anthology/aquinas40.htm

118. See Web Site: http://byzantinecalvinist.blogspot.com/2003_10_01_byzantinecalvinist_archive.html

119. Bill Haynes, *Just War Theory and Iraq*, in ACLJ, American Center for Law and Justice, Web Site: http://www.aclj.org/news/bibpers/020917_preemptive.asp

120. Including the so-called 'swinging six' countries, (non-permanent members of the UNSC), which were Pakistan, Chili, Mexico, Cameroon, Angola and Guinea

121. Walter B. Slocombe, *Force, Pre-emption and Legitimacy*, in Survival (The IISS Quarterly, Volume 45, Number 1, Spring 2003), p. 125

122. See Web Site: http://www.wand.org/9-11/justwar.html

CHAPTER SIX

123. Jean de la Fontaine, *Fables*, (Ed. J. Dupuis Fils & Co, Marcinelle-Charleroi, Belgique, 1970), p. 80

124. George Patton, General, http://www.cs.virginia.edu/~robins/quotes.html

125. D.J. Harris, op. cit., p. 1056

126. David A. Hamburg and Cyrus R. Vance, *Preventing Deadly Conflicts*, (Carnegie Corporation of New York, 1997), p. 41

127. Ibid., p. 49

128. Sun Tzu, *The Art of War*, translated by Samuel B. Griffith, (Oxford University Press, UK, 1963), p 77

129. David A. Hamburg and Cyrus R. Vance, op. cit., p. 52

130. Ibid., p. 59

131. Military use of force as 'ultimate resort' describes the most extreme and unpleasant action which has to be implemented if other resorts, such as diplomatic efforts and economic sanctions, are exhausted.

132. David A. Hamburg and Cyrus R. Vance, op. cit., p. 62

133. Several UN resolutions to the Iraq - Kuwait case, beginning with UN Resolution 660; UN Resolution 678 of November 29th 1990 formally authorised the use of military force by January 15th 1991. See also the UN resolutions web site: http://

ods-dds-ny.un.org/doc/RESOLUTION/GEN/NR0/575/10/
IMG/NR057510.pdf?OpenElement

See also http://ods-dds- ny.un.org/doc/RESOLUTION/GEN/
NR0/575/28/IMG/NR057528.pdf?OpenElement

134. UN Resolution 1373 stipulates, amongst other things, the
need to combat by all means, in accordance with the UNC,
threats to international peace and security and to take the
necessary steps to prevent the commission of terrorist acts;
these sentences formally authorized the use of military against
the Taliban regime of Afghanistan. See also the UN resolutions web site: http://ods-dds-ny.un.org/doc/UNDOC/GEN/
N01/557/43/PDF/N0155743.pdf?OpenElement

135. _____, *The United States: Changed Utterly?*, in Strategic
Survey 2002/2003, op. cit., p. 70

136. Walter B. Slocombe, op. cit., p. 118

137. Ibid., p. 124

138. Hans Bachofner, *Versäumte Chancen, Sicherheitspolitik
nach dem 11. September 2001*, Schweizerzeit-Schriftenreihe Nr.
40, (Schweizerzeit Verlags AG, 8416 Flaach, Switzerland, April
2002), p. 6

139. Ibid., p. 6

140. Robert S. Litwak, op. cit., p. 53

141. Ibid., p. 53

142. _____, *The United States: Changed Utterly?*, in Strategic
Survey 2002/2003, op. cit., p. 71

143. US President's State of the Union address on January 29th
2002; See White House web site: http://www.whitehouse.gov/
news/releases/2002/01/20020129-11.html

144. The White House, *A National Strategy for a New Century*, (The White House, December 1999), pp. 19-20; See also White House Web site on: http://www.dtic.mil/doctrine/jel/other_pubs/nssr99.pdf

145. Walter B. Slocombe, op. cit., p. 119

146. Ibid., p. 120

147. Ibid., pp. 119-120

148. Hans Bachofner, op. cit., p. 7

149. Ibid., p. 7

150. Carl von Clausewitz, *Vom Kriege*, translated as On War by Michael Howard and Peter Paret, (Princeton University Press, Princeton NJ, 1976), p. 198

151. White House Web site: http://www.whitehouse.gov/news/releases/2002/06/20020601-3.html

152. John Hughes-Wilson, *Military Intelligence Blunders*, (Constable Publishers, London, 1999), p. 5

153. Loch K. Johnson, *Secret Agencies: U.S. Intelligence in a Hostile World*, (Yale University Press, USA, 1996), p. 4

154. The Schlesinger Working Group on Strategic Surprises, ISD; See Web Site: http://cfdev.georgetown.edu/sfs/programs/isd/schlesinger/

155. John Hughes-Wilson, op. cit., p. 10

156. Ibid., p. 13

157. Jacques Baud, *La Guerre Assymétrique ou la Défaite du Vainqueur*, (L'Art de la Guerre, Editions du Rocher, Paris, 2003), p. 163

158. Ibid., p. 163

159. Ali Hassan al-Majid earned the nickname Chemical Ali for masterminding chemical attacks on Iraqi Kurds in 1988. On one occasion, he rejected suggestions he had killed 182,000 people with the chilling reply: 'No, it could not have been more than 100,000.'... His most infamous outrage was the use of poison gas to kill scores of Kurds at Halabaja in 1988. But Kurds were not the only target of his ruthless ruling style - any opponent of the regime was a potential target. (Talk garnered from BBC Night News on BBC Two, June 6th 2003, 22h45)

160. _____, *Iraq's Weapons of Mass Destruction*, The Assessment of the British Government, (The Stationery Office Limited, London, 2002), p. 19

161. BBC News on BBC One, June 8th 2003, 16h45

162. _____, *Iraq's Weapons of Mass Destruction*, *The Assessment of the British Government*, op. cit., p. 6

163. James M. Poland, *Understanding Terrorism, Groups, Strategies and Responses*, (Prentice-Hall, Inc., New Jersey, USA, 1988), p. 195

164. Jeff Nesmith, *US Satellite Eavesdroppers Seek Needles in Global Haystack*, (Cox News, Washington Bureau, 7.10.2001). See also Web site: http://www.coxnews.com/washingtonbureau/staff/nesmith/100701TER-ECHELON.html

165. Bruce Hoffman, *Old Madness, New Methods*, (Rand Review Winter 1998-99), p. 19 See also Web site: http://www.rand.org/publications/randreview/issues/rrwinter98.9.pdf

166. In the speech by Prime Minister Tony Blair at the TUC Conference on September 10th 2002.

167. *Amnesty International's 10-point appeal*; See web site: http://www.amnesty.org.nz/web/Pages/home.nsf/dd5cab6801

f1723588256474005327c8/d04e52d0f0188875cc256d1d001e2b
89!OpenDocument

168. Ibid.

169. Jacques Baud, op. cit., p. 164

170. Ibid., p. 164

171. The White House, *National Security Strategy of the United States of America*, (The White House, September 17th 2002). See also Web site: http://www.whitehouse.gov/nsc/nss.html

172. Walter B. Slocombe, op. cit., p. 126

173. Ibid., p. 126

174. Ibid., pp. 126-127

175. Abstract of Chapter 5 of the US NSS: '...The nature of the Cold War threat required the United States - with our allies and friends - to emphasize deterrence of the enemy's use of force, producing a grim strategy of mutual assured destruction. With the collapse of the Soviet Union and the end of the Cold War, our security environment has undergone profound transformation. ... But new deadly challenges have emerged from rogue states and terrorists. None of these contemporary threats rival the sheer destructive power that was arrayed against us by the Soviet Union. However, the nature and motivations of these new adversaries, their determination to obtain destructive powers hitherto available only to the world's strongest states, and the greater likelihood that they will use weapons of mass destruction against us, make today's security environment more complex and dangerous.' See also White House Web Site: http://www.whitehouse.gov/nsc/nss5.html

176. Lawrence Freedman, op. cit., p. 110

CHAPTER SEVEN

177. Carl von Clausewitz, op. cit., p. 78

178. Lawrence Freedman, op. cit., p. 107

179. *Cobuild, English Dictionary for Advanced Learners*, op. cit., p. 781

180. Christine Gray, op. cit., p. 119

181. Ibid., p. 119

182. D.J. Harris, op. cit., p. 897

183. James M. Poland, op. cit., p. 199

184. Guy Millière, *Ce que veut Bush, La recomposition du monde*, (Editions de La Martinière, France, 2003), p. 143

185. Ibid., p. 153

186. Ibid., p.157

187. See web site: http://www.whitehouse.gov/news/releases/2002/09/20020911-3.html